Tales of the Anglers Rest

by
Patricia Armstrong

MAVERICK

First published in the UK 1995 by Maverick Sporting Publications
an imprint of Midlands MAC (PUBLISHING)
65 St. Giles Street, Northampton NN1 1JF

Copyright © 1995

All rights reserved. No part of this book may be reproduced or transmitted in any form or by any means, electronic or mechanical, including photo-copying, recording or any information storage and retrieval system, without permission in writing from the copyright holder and publisher.

British Library Cataloguing-in-Publication Data.
A catalogue record for this title is available from the British Library.

ISBN 1 899078 04 5

Typeset by Midlands MAC
Northampton NN1 1JF
Printed and bound in Great Britain by
J.B. Offset Printers (Marks Tey) Ltd.
Marks Tey, Colchester, Essex

FOREWORD

During the course of this year I've skimmed through a number of fishing books, for it is my job to decide whether they are going to be sellers or not. If my judgment is wrong I can assure you as a book wholesaler it is very bad for business.

Being involved with game fishing so closely for more years than I care to add up, I feel I know a good thing when I see it. I also feel I know our author Patricia Armstrong after reading her absorbing manuscript. From the stories she tells of her and her husband James' fishing experiences, I have travelled a similar path in life as they have.

To be honest bedside fishing story books have become unfashionable over the last twenty years, but I feel most confident this one will be the first to reverse that trend. The book is written with good humour and is bound to make you smile, while the big fish encounters are exciting enough to give the reader a feeling of 'being there'.

Both Pat and James have two sporting loves which have taken up most of their spare time since they were married, golf and fishing. James even sneaked his fishing kit along on their honeymoon many years ago and caught a salmon. Pat decided she would have a go after seeing James land a 12 pounder and the excitement that followed back at the little hotel. The whole scene appealed to her and soon she caught her first salmon. The rest you will read about in the chapters of this book.

As Pat says "It was quite by chance I became a writer." First she wrote a series of stories to amuse a sick friend, who later showed them to Max Hastings who suggested they should be sent to national fishing magazines. These were published by Trout & Salmon, The Field and Salmon, Trout & Seatrout magazines.

These days Pat and James spend a couple of days a week fishing for the rainbow trout of Enton Lakes which is close to their home. However they still manage a few trips for salmon and they wouldn't miss their nine holes of golf. Equal sporting interests is obviously a very good thing for a happy marriage.

Bob Church
Northampton

*For James
In celebration of
all the good years*

CONTENTS

Tirra Lirra by the River	7
First Salmon	13
Suzie	27
Rocky	35
A proper Big Fish	39
The one that got away	45
Trouble with waders	53
Posthumous Salmon	57
The downfall of Old Charlie	63
What are you doing down there?	69
Runaway boat	73
Worms	79
The cold cure	85
Any Luck?	93
Etiquette	99
Merry as the marriage bell	107
The angler's curse	113
Not enough action	119
Life begins at Sixty-five	127
The Colonel's Thousandth	133
Night fishing for Sea Trout	139
Sea Trout by day	145
Hypothermia	151
Nearly another monument	159
A day on a chalk stream	163
Lake Rainbow	171
Losing Salmon	177
The Devil's Bait	183
Always the big one	189
Halcyon Day	197
The Bob Fly	201

Tirra Lirra by the River

When I say we had no honeymoon, that is not strictly true. Our post-wedding holiday was delayed until we could find time to get away from work and London.

James made all the arrangements, and one Saturday we set off for the wilds of Wales, ultimately arriving at our hotel near Llanfihangel-ar-Arth.

Secreted in the boot of the car there was a trout rod, a small box containing flies, a reel, spare spools, casts and a pair of thigh waders. "Just in case we find a decent bit of river," explained James.

I must have been very naive in those days: of course there was a river, and the hotel was basically a rather refined species of fishing pub which he had specially selected from a publication, well known to the cognoscenti, titled 'Where to Fish'.

Still besotted with my new husband, after tea I followed him down to the banks of the Teifi, where we made a quick reconnaissance. I knew absolutely nothing about fishing and didn't particularly want to learn. I pictured myself sitting quietly on the river bank, watching the water and the wildlife, reading a book in the open air and generally relaxing. But no, with James one has to be active; sitting down is a waste of time and, when fishing is possible, a sacrilege. We had been there less than an hour when he had his rod up and, with a bit of red wool tied on the leader to represent a fly, was teaching me to cast in a secluded meadow behind the hotel.

Sunday morning dawned fine and clear and immediately after breakfast we set out for the river bank. Emma, James' golden retriever, fully understood about fishing and she was in a state of high excitement. In about half a mile we came to what James pronounced to be a promising run. Clambering through nettles and brambles, he slipped quietly into the water.

Emma had no difficulty with the river bank at all: in London she fitted in with our lives, but here she was like a liberated spirit. As we walked she rolled ecstatically in the lush grass, pounced on real and imaginary creatures on the river bank and swam enthusiastically in pursuit of water voles. Once fishing had begun, however, she sat on the bank, almost in the river and, never taking her eyes off James, she waited.

After about fifteen minutes James exclaimed 'I've just risen a fish."

He went back a few paces and stood absolutely still for five minutes, and then started casting again. Emma was now trembling with anticipation and I wondered what they were both getting so agitated about.

Suddenly there was a great cry "Yes." The rod bent double and the battle was on. James waded rapidly downstream, his reel screaming. Emma leapt to her feet and followed him down the bank. Even I cantered up and down, although I had no idea what was on the end of the line.

Then, out of the water jumped a beautiful silver fish, flashing in the sunlight, with drops like pearls streaming from him as he thrashed his tail in the air. I found that I was holding my breath and praying for him to stay on.

James, hoarse with excitement, called to me "We've no net. Come down here and give me your handkerchief, I've dropped mine."

Since I had recently promised to obey, I fought my way through all the natural hazards, getting pricked and stung in the process, and managed to hand him my precious lace-edged hankie, although I couldn't see what use a small wisp of material was going to be in the circumstances. It hardly seemed the right time to complain about my wet feet either.

After some twenty heart-stopping minutes of frenzied activity, the fish was tired and lying on its side in the clear water James wrapped the handkerchief round his hand and gently, oh so gently, picked the fish up by the tail and leapt several feet backwards.

"Take the rod. Take the rod," he cried, carrying the flapping fish well up the bank to safety. He killed it quickly and neatly with a couple of blows from an instrument which looked to me like a small knobkerry, explaining that it was called a priest, because it was used to deliver the last rites.

We fished on for the rest of the morning without further incident and then made our way back to the hotel for lunch. Secretive by nature, we crept into the hotel garage-cum-rod room and put the fish on the slab. James shed his waders, since it was not the sort of establishment that encouraged messy fishermen with muddy waders into the main building.

We changed and went for a pre-lunch drink. The lounge was full of elderly fishermen consuming whiskies and pink gins. The slightly superior landlord asked politely if we had had a good morning.

"Got one nice fish," said James casually. "About twelve."

"Twelve ounces, that's not a bad trout for this river," remarked our host.

"Wasn't ounces," said James.

We were given our sherries and the landlord occupied himself with one of the other residents, but suddenly stopped and turned back to us.

"What did you say?" he demanded.

"I said it wasn't ounces, and it wasn't a trout, it was a fish," said James, a trifle pedantically.

"But you only had a trout rod and trout flies."

"Yes," agreed James.

"And you had no net."

"No net," confirmed James nonchalantly.

By this time everyone was listening to the landlord and the newcomer.

"Where is it?" asked the landlord, rather suspiciously.

"In the garage, on the slab," said James, sipping his Bristol Cream with some satisfaction.

I have never seen a bar empty so quickly: everyone rushed to the garage to view the catch. In about ten minutes they all returned, demanding full details of the event and plying us with drinks. It appeared that salmon were mostly caught on the worm on that river, and hooking one on a fly, let alone a small trout fly, was an achievement of some magnitude.

For the rest of our stay we were treated with deference, which I found extremely embarrassing seeing that I knew less than nothing about fishing. James gave me a crash course in the names of flies, breaking strains of nylon and other essential angling lore so that I could at least look intelligent.

Although there were sea trout in the river, no-one, it seemed, ever fished at night. James and Emma did. After dinner they went down to the bridge pool, just in front of the hotel, as dusk was falling. The first night they arrived back after a couple of hours, James carrying several nice sea trout and highly indignant. The hotel was illuminated by a spotlight switched on by the landlord after dark - all very picturesque, but apparently that night when the light came on the reflection lit up the pool, up to then a hive of activity, and all the fish promptly went down. Thereafter, when James went out to fish at night the front of' the hotel remained in darkness.

As the week went by the weather became finer and the river lower, so that there was rather less activity during the day. We would hurry breakfast and be out on the bank as early as possible, before the day got too bright and hot. James caught another salmon and I actually landed my first sea trout. Naturally I was delighted when my husband suggested that we tour the countryside and I thought that perhaps I had misjudged him and that my charms were at least equal to those of salmo salar and salmo trutta. I should have known better; the 'tour of the countryside' included practically every tackle shop within a twenty mile radius, but we did acquire, among other things, a net.

Deserted after dinner each evening, I resorted to works from the hotel bookcase. I found an absolute gem, edited by a Mr Dickie, called 'Great Angling Stories. Of its many wonderful tales, the one I liked best was 'Angler's Wives' by C.R. Green.

It appeared that the young, newly-wed Mrs Trimble was horrified by the methods employed by the middle-aged, fisherman-weary Mrs Benson to punish her fanatical husband. The poor man's waders were pierced with a bodkin so that his feet were constantly damp from a slow leak, and a small boy was bribed to swim in the best pool of his beat just before he was due to fish there. Mrs Benson cut some strands of his net, substituted an old, brittle cast for his new one or touched his line with a flame so that it broke at the most crucial moment. Eventually, however, young Mrs Trimble broke down and, incensed by her husband's neglect on their honeymoon, she asked to borrow the bodkin.

I know exactly how she must have felt. Perhaps it is just as well I had not read the story earlier, or it might have put ideas into my head. As it happens, events took quite a different turn so that instead of becoming a fishing widow I became, as so often is the case with converts, a fishing addict. But that is, as they say, another story.

First Salmon

In spring, when the water is high and the temperature low, I usually carry both fly and spinning rods. I prefer to fish with a fly if possible, but being quite small does mean that the water I can cover wading with a fly rod is often limited. Tucking myself into corners and under trees with an 8ft spinning rod and a fixed-spool reel - places inaccessible to the fly - has produced unexpected fish over the years and some friendly chagrin from other members of the party. Spinning itself is an art and should not be despised. Standing under a tree, or with a sheer bank behind, a flick of the wrist can put a bait accurately against the far bank of all but the largest rivers. That I have sometimes found myself playing fish in very tricky circumstances and have required help from nearby and more orthodox anglers is indisputable, but it all adds to the fascination of salmon fishing.

I am ashamed to say that I did not succeed in landing the first salmon I ever hooked. It was lost through a combination of inexperience and over-excitement. When the fish first showed, James was fishing alone; I was just upstream at the tail of the pool above. For some time he had been determined that I should catch a salmon and, altruistic character that he can be on rare occasions, he rushed to tell me to reel in and come quickly.

It was the sort of pool that began in a cascade over great slabs of rock, below which the water boiled in a cauldron so that there was an enormous whirlpool and anything cast in there was at once sucked under. Some ten paces below, the water became calmer with a nice fast run. It was an easy place from which to fish with a flat, shingle bank.

"Use your spinning, rod," said James. "It's not possible to hold a fly over his lie. See, there, just where the current begins, below the white water. I saw him head-and-tail only a few minutes ago. Throw your minnow well downstream and to the far side and let it come across his nose. I'm sure it's a taking fish."

I had caught trout, both brown and rainbow, and quite sizeable sea trout, but this was the big one and I was nervous about the whole project. It seemed to me that as we wanted to catch a salmon and James knew where the fish was and exactly how to approach it, then he should do it himself. I offered him my spinning rod, but he was adamant that I should try.

On the third cast the fish rose again, head-and-tail. "Probably at you," said James. "But the water is so fast that he missed it. Wait for two minutes, let him settle and then try again."

Two casts later the salmon took me with a bang and promptly made off downstream. And then, tragedy. I was using an Abu closed face, fixed-spool reel, which I love dearly and still use, but if the handle is turned back, even fractionally, with a fish on it locks the spool. In the heat of the moment I must have touched the handle and the spool locked. Something had to give; the 18 pound nylon snapped with a loud crack and I was left grieving.

Nothing else happened that day, and it was my considered opinion that I did not deserve to catch a salmon and probably never would. I felt the loss keenly and was thoroughly miserable.

Next day, however, the river gods were in forgiving vein. I was fishing a nice pool with a high bank on our side and a convenient shingle bottom. When it became too deep to wade, I climbed out of the water and changed my fly rod for my spinning rod, loaded with a small Devon minnow. I was then able to continue down the pool by edging my way along a rudimentary shelf at the bottom of the bank, just above the water. James, who had already been down the pool with a Thunder and Lightning, was sitting half way up the bank behind me, well off the skyline, perched on some exposed tree roots, quietly contemplating the contents of his fly box. I had snagged several times on a grassy shelf on the opposite bank, which was just under the water. I snagged again and gave a bad-tempered tug; the minnow came free and sank into the current.

Just as I was about to wind, James gave a great cry from his vantage point above me. "Fish!" He had looked up when I snagged and exclaimed in annoyance, just in time to see a large salmon rise from its lie against the opposite bank and engulf my minnow as it sank. The line stopped, tightened and moved away quite slowly. James slithered down to my side, exhorting me not to touch the reel.

With the previous day's disaster still very fresh in my memory I kept my hand well away from the handle. "Keep the rod up," urged James. "Don't point it at the fish."

This time he was taking no chances, but made me ease the tension by loosening the clutch a little. Finally, realising that he was hooked, the salmon ran, fast upstream.

"Follow him," cried James. "Go on, woman. Follow."

I did, until I had run out of bank and was hesitating about taking to the water, but he practically pushed me in. Once my thigh waders were full there seemed little point in not going the whole hog. The salmon continued to take line and I waded after him as fast as I could, the bow-wave now waist high. When he came to the fast water at the head of the pool he checked, moving from side to side in the strong current. James, who had followed me in the comfort of his chest waders, came to my side.

"Now you can tighten the clutch a little. Keep the rod up and let him work against the current, that'll help to tire him."

Twice the salmon nearly made it through the twenty yards of white water into the pool above, then slowly he started to come back towards me. I recovered line when I could, but still kept my left hand well clear of the reel whenever he moved away.

I had seen those spectacular films of salmon running, outlined against great walls of water and leaping up seemingly impossible weirs, but nothing had prepared me for the awesome power of the creature when tethered to the end of a fishing line. I had certainly not anticipated the sheer strength of a fresh-run spring salmon, and there were times when I doubted that I could hold on to the rod much longer. The playing of that fish seemed to take forever, and all the time I was in terror of losing him.

At last the great fish began to come to the surface, making huge eddies and swirls, and then to roll so that his belly showed white.

"Nearly done now," said James, checking his tailer. "Start taking in line very slowly. Point the rod in towards the bank to bring him to this side."

Nearer and nearer came the fish, and I held my breath. "Gently, very gently," murmured James. "Wait until he's right on his side, then he won't try to run when he sees us."

Sure enough, the salmon finally rolled on his side and came slowly to our feet. The tailer went home and James quickly dragged him flapping up the bank and safely into the field beyond.

As the magnificent fish lay on the grass, for one mad moment I wanted to return it to its element, to set it free, but the urge passed swiftly and the priest was used.

"Lovely fish," said James with relief. "Best part of 20 pounds. Sea lice with tails. Well done. Exactly thirty-eight minutes since you first hooked him."

I had seen salmon caught before, but this one, all 18 pounds of him, was mine. He was dipped in the river at hourly intervals and thoroughly washed so that the skin would not wrinkle, and at the end of the day I bore him back to the hotel, where he was proudly displayed on the huge hall plate.

An old angler in the party said that no matter how long I lived, or how many salmon I caught, I would always remember that day. He was quite right. even today, many years and my fair share of salmon later, I can close my eyes and be transported back to that pool; I can see the great trees leaning out over the water, can feel the slippery bank under my feet and know the exact taking place. My acute anxiety while playing him still comes back to me, and I remember that I felt so weak afterwards that I had to sit down on the bank to recover.

I defy anyone who has ever caught salmon with rod and line to forget any detail of the capture of their first.

Definitely not a virtue

Whenever fishing is being discussed, someone can be relied upon to remark that they wouldn't have the patience. Since this is the very last attribute required for game fishing, whether on river or still water, mention of it tends to make even the mildest angler annoyed. The implication is that he, or she, sits on a comfortable grassy tussock on the bank, watching a float to signal any activity below the surface.

While it is true that if one keeps still and quiet there are many things to be seen on a river bank, from a boat or by a lakeside, actually fishing for trout or salmon requires specialised knowledge, skill, stamina, agility, concentration and a high degree of stoicism, taking place as it often does in the foulest weather.

All the sights and sounds of water and its surroundings are an added bonus to the fisherman. I have seen a grass snake swim across a strong current, mink climb trees, herons fishing at the water's edge, cormorants drying their huge wings in the sun, and dippers appearing to walk under the water. A kingfisher perched on James' rod tip on one occasion.

There are birds, butterflies, electric blue damsel flies, iridescent dragonflies, water voles, frogs, beetles, wild flowers and a million other things to be enjoyed.

Tinker, a retired sea captain, took up fishing rather later in life than most. He had been foolhardy enough to say in the hearing of addicted anglers that he was not blessed with sufficient patience to fish, although water, be it sea, river or lake, was essential to life as far as he was concerned.

His friends fell on him, extolling the virtues, the excitement, the activity involved in the sport. With his wife, he was enrolled for a course of casting lessons, and they both conquered the technical difficulties in no time at all. Of course, once having landed their first trout they were hooked for all time.

After a season of good trout fishing, Tinker and Margaret were ready to embark upon their first salmon fishing trip with us to the West Country. James checked all their equipment, gave them short lectures on what to do in any eventuality, and off we all went.

The river was high and coloured, it was windy and cold, with occasional snow flurries. Certainly it was not fly water at the beginning of the holiday, so we armed ourselves with spinning rods.

Tinker and Margaret were excited, but nervous, and they kept very close to us.

During the first morning, James hooked a fish in a difficult place and, in following it downstream, he came to the end of the bank. Here he found himself against a large tree and he could go no further, but the fish could, and did.

Hearing the great bellow from upstream, Tinker and Margaret came rushing along the bank to see their first salmon caught. They stood mesmerised by the sight of the fish jumping in the pool, then tearing downstream.

"Don't just stand there," shouted James. "Lie down on that rock and I'll try to bring him in so that you can tail him for me."

Tinker looked absolutely terrified, but he did as he was told without a word. I was already lying down on another part of the bank, tailer in hand, ready to get the fish if he came anywhere near me.

"Margaret" James called. "Come and take my net and go round the corner in case he comes to you there."

Margaret was petrified and for a moment I thought she was going to run away, the responsibility too great to bear, but she took the net and made off downstream and out of sight round the corner.

After several false alarms, the salmon finally tired and lay on its side, near Tinker. A large man, he stretched out an arm the size of a small tree trunk, put the tailer round the salmon and heaved it out of the water in a cloud of spray.

Fortunately James had let the line loose on the reel because Tinker, remembering James' instructions about getting a salmon well away from the water in case it escaped back to its natural element, stumbled to his feet, took to his heels and, clutching the fish to his chest, didn't stop until he was forty yards into the field behind.

We found him on his knees, wrestling with the slippery salmon, the tailer and yards of nylon.

'My God," he whispered, ashen faced, "I'd never manage that on my own. You'd better stay close in case we hook something."

The water gradually subsided to near its normal level and the fishing was good. Tinker and Margaret had several nice sea trout, all about four pounds, but no salmon. They were enjoying themselves immensely.

One day, towards the end of our stay, James and I had both triumphed and decided in the early evening to carry our fish across the field to our car. There had been no sign of Tinker and Margaret since having lunch with them in the hut and we assumed that they had gone back to the hotel, particularly since they had become more proficient and independent during the week and had taken to wandering off on their own.

We all bathed, dressed for dinner and gathered in the bar for pre-prandials, when we realised that Tinker and Margaret had not put in an appearance. James was dismayed. "We'll have to go and look for them," he said. "Something must have happened."

At that moment they hove into sight. Through the window we could see the happy, exhausted, muddy pair. They were unloading a large salmon from the boot of their car.

The bar emptied. We surrounded them, exclaiming over the fish and ushering them into the hall, where it was weighed and displayed on the slab - fifteen pounds of shining silver. We ordered two large gins, which we thrust into their hands with instructions to take their drinks upstairs with them, have a quick bath and change and then come down and tell us all about it.

Later they arrived to join us in the bar, glowing with pride, gin and pleasure at the prospect of recounting the tale. There were two distinctly different versions of the story, but we were inclined to put more credence on Margaret's reconstruction.

After lunch, they had fished down to the lowest beat which, at their rate of progress had taken them until early evening.

"Shall we go home now?" asked Tinker, "Or shall we go over 'Upper Bridge Pool' again, just for luck?"

Margaret had agreed that they should fish for another half-hour before packing up for the day. She had started to fish a nice easy run, just upstream, while Tinker started down the main pool. The wading was not difficult, shallow at the edges with a high bank behind.

About two-thirds of the way down the pool Tinker hooked a fish. Trying desperately to remember all he had been told, he called to Margaret to reel in and come immediately.

"Get out of the water if possible," James had said. Well, he couldn't because of the high bank. "Get downstream of the fish." He had difficulty with that one too because he didn't want to risk the fish running under one arch of the bridge.

Tinker stood his ground, reeling in line when he could, until the salmon's rushes became less frantic. It was a particularly obliging fish because at no time did it try to go downstream and through the bridge.

The salmon was obviously getting tired after about twenty minutes, and Tinker succeeded in freeing his tailer from its string around his back in readiness for the moment of truth.

Suddenly the line went dead; there was no movement at all. Tinker stood there for several long moments. Nothing. The fish must have got round a snag and escaped.

Furious in his disappointment, Tinker gave tongue, releasing all the poetry learned in a lifetime at sea. He flung the tailer over his head, over the high bank and into the field beyond. All his pent-up nautical repertoire disturbed the air around them, while Margaret stood, impotent and in tears, on the bank.

When he had at last exhausted himself and his exotic vocabulary, Tinker decided that at least he must retrieve his bait from the snag. Wading in as far as he dared, reeling in line as he went, he gave a couple of sharp jerks to try to free his minnow.

He was quite unprepared for what happened next. There was a quivering 'Thump' on the end of the line and the salmon exploded out of the water. It was still on.

After its little rest at the bottom of the river, the salmon had taken a new lease on life. It ran upstream, it jumped and it plunged. At last it was tired and started to roll on the surface.

"Bring me the tailer. Quickly!" he shouted to Margaret "Quickly!"

Margaret scampered off into the field to retrieve the tailer, but it was nowhere to be seen, lost in the long grass. It was her turn to give vent to her feelings, and she stood there, hurling abuse at Tinker.

Meanwhile, the salmon was getting another rest; it had managed to swim sluggishly a few yards into the river, where it went nose down again.

Tinker waded in after it, still uttering expletives. He could see the fish clearly in the pellucid water, nose down and tail up, only about a foot under the surface. With the utmost caution,so as not to panic the salmon into taking off again, he approached it from behind. Without pausing to roll up his sleeve or remove his watch, he plunged his arm in and grasped the fish firmly above the tail, as he had been instructed as an emergency measure should he ever find himself without net or tailer.

Tinker stumbled upstream, bearing the rod in one hand and the flapping fish in the other. There was no way he could get up the high bank and out of the river, so he splashed his way up to the shingle, making a wave like a destroyer.

Once on the level stony bank, he put the rod down safely and fell on the fish. Margaret was ordered to find the priest in his pocket, while he kept a firm hold on his precious salmon. So convinced was he that with one bound it would free itself and make for the river again that he ordered Margaret to deliver the coup de grâce. With her first sighting shot she missed the fish completely, catching Tinker a painful blow on the knuckles.

There was more colourful language. With her second blow she succeeded in dispatching the salmon to piscatorial paradise.

With the fish safely dead and well away from the river, they had spent another twenty minutes or so searching for the missing tailer.

As we were about to go in to dinner, a couple of non-angling guests arrived for an over-night stay.

"What a splendid sight," said the wife, looking at Tinker's salmon on the hall slab. "But I would never have enough patience to fish."

"Patience be damned,' growled Tinker like a veteran. "That's the very last thing you need."

Suzie

"Beef to the heel, like a Mullingar heifer," said our friend unkindly. "An absolute menace on the river bank. Clumsy. Scares every fish for miles. She came with us once. Never again. Just as I was concentrating on my casting she would come crashing out of the undergrowth and stand on the skyline. Hopeless. Never catches anything, of course."

It is true that Suzie is a strapping girl and perhaps not quite as well co-ordinated as some, but she has a sweet and generous nature and loves being out in the country, preferably near water. She was most enthusiastic about joining our party for some autumn sea trout and salmon fishing, although it remains a mystery how she came to be included, since nobody has ever admitted to having invited her. I felt sure that our friend's picture of her must be overdrawn; it was just not possible to be that bad. She seemed to me to be well equipped for a river - enough ballast to keep her steady in a current and tall enough to make wading easy. I was wrong.

Suzie was assigned to me on the first day. She had never seen that particular river before, but I knew the water intimately. As we walked our beat I pointed out the pools and where fish usually lay. Trying to be quiet, she spoke in a stage whisper until I assured her that fish cannot hear voices, they only register vibrations, footsteps, grating on stones, splashing, that sort of thing. She clomped along behind me, tripping over tree roots and brambles and getting caught up on spiky branches. Poor girl, I thought, she is so used to being reprimanded about her blunderings that she is inhibited. If I just show her the best places to fish and leave her alone she can relax and all will be well. Wrong again.

By the end of the day my nerves were in tatters and my own fly had spent very little time in the water. We had been up trees retrieving her flies; we had spent ages undoing some quite astonishing tangles in her cast - or should I say casts, since she seemed also to have exhausted my entire supply for the week - and we had on several occasions to empty her waders and wring out her socks. At the end of the afternoon, no doubt worn out by her efforts, she tripped and fell over backwards in the shallows. She grinned, shamefaced, and said she loved fishing but somehow she always had little accidents. But anyway, wasn't it wonderful just to be out in the country and on the river. Catching fish would be a bonus, of course, but just being there was enough.

I ground my teeth silently and suggested that we make our way home to dry out.

James arrived back to the hotel just in time to change for dinner. He had had a good day, with a brace of salmon and some sea trout, and he was in expansive mood. Wasn't the river in perfect condition? Just the right colour after the rain for sea trout and a good run of salmon. I was less enchanted; it had taken several very necessary drinks to dull the pain of Suzie and the day's events. However, I was still sufficiently alert to employ my feminine guile to persuade James to agree to take her in hand. Benign after a pleasantly successful day and some rather good claret, he said he would be delighted to show her the top beat tomorrow.

My husband has many excellent qualities, but suffering fools gladly is not one of them. On arrival home the next evening I knew what to expect because the landlord said James had demanded a bottle and a small tumbler and had gone straight upstairs, fulminating. I found him lying in a hot bath, glass in hand. His trousers, jumper and socks were in a muddy pile on a sheet of polythene; his underclothes were soaking in the washbasin. I asked, as gently as possible, if he felt able to talk about it. "Just," he said bitterly.

The morning had been totally disrupted from the fishing point of view, but it was as nothing to the afternoon. Their real troubles had started after lunch with an incident involving a small herd of bullocks.

It must be pretty boring being a bullock, with nothing to do but graze all day, which is why they welcome little interludes of activity. This particular group had certainly found Suzie attractive and interesting. James shooed them away several times, telling her that they were harmless, just naturally inquisitive, and that the worst they were likely to do was to lick anything left lying about. If she ignored them they would leave her alone. When this profound piece of advice failed, James suggested that she sit quietly on the bank and read her book for half-an-hour. With Suzie settled, James drove the bullocks away into the field and returned to the river.

Until then it had been impossible to concentrate on his own fishing, but now, mercifully, Suzie was out of his hair, if only temporarily, and he could put his mind to the business in hand. He was half way down a pool when a salmon rose, head-and-tail, just downstream of him. He was working his way towards the fish when there was a great cry "Help me!"

Cursing, James reeled in and sped to the source of the commotion. While Suzie had been sitting reading her book, the bullocks had surrounded her, silently, like ghosts. The first indication she had of their presence was when one actually leaned against her and licked her neck.

A bullock's tongue is hot and wet and curiously rough, and the effect of its attentions on Suzie was electric. She leapt to her feet, dropping her book, which plummeted down the bank into the river; she then attempted to climb a tree which overhung the water precariously.

It was here that James found her, terrified out of her wits, while the bullocks stared with tremendous interest at the spectacle. He drove the intruders off and helped the poor girl to terra firma. She insisted on accompanying him back to his pool, saying that she would sit quietly on the bank to watch him fish. She promised to keep well off the skyline, to be absolutely still and quiet, like a mouse; he wouldn't know she was there, but she wanted to stay with him in case the beasts came back again.

James waded into the pool and worked out line. The salmon rose again, head-and-tail, a taking fish for certain, he thought.

He made his way quickly down towards the place, and so absorbed was he that he failed to notice that Suzie had moved.

He had just decided that the next cast should do it, when Suzie and about a ton of earth arrived in the river dead opposite the fish. On seeing the fish rise, Suzie had become very excited and had crawled on hands and knees along the bank to get a better view. Unfortunately she had not realised that the bank was eroded and corniced, and it had given way under her considerable weight at the crucial moment.

In the process of rescuing Suzie from the river, James had suffered almost total immersion himself. They were both covered in mud and very wet. "And do you know what that wretched girl did?" said James savagely. "She stood on the bank, giggling. She said we were both in such a mess that the only way to get cleaned up was to go skinny dipping. She found the whole thing amusing. No word of apology, and every fish in the pool probably making for the sea."

And so the week wore on, each of us taking it in turn to look after Suzie, and none enjoying the experience. On the third day the inevitable happened: she had committed the unforgivable sin of leaving her rod flat on the bank and, not looking where she was going, had stepped back, crushing the tip. We found her an old fibreglass rod, the least valuable of all the spares carried by members of the party in case of accident. James found her a spool of extra-strong nylon to use for casts and we all contributed to the replenishment of her depleted fly box. She caught nothing, but did learn to take a towel and a change of clothes to the fishing hut so that there was no need to return to the hotel when she fell in.

Finally it was Guy's turn. We had left him to last in the hope that Suzie would improve sufficiently under our tutelage to cause minimum upset to his sensibilities, for he is, of all our fishing companions, the most finely tuned. He is excessively careful, not to say pernickety. Pedantic about tackle, methods of angling and river lore, I have known him to take a full fifteen minutes to wade quietly into a pool. In his opinion, in fishing the approach is everything. He insists that peace and quiet are of paramount importance on a river; the angler must try to achieve 'oneness' with his surroundings. Nobody dares to speak to him on a river bank for fear of disturbing his concentration.

While we did not feel that Suzie had progressed sufficiently for Guy, we had each put up with her and it was now his turn. By this time the river had cleared so that the shy sea trout were not to be caught by day, but there were still salmon about. Guy prepared his ground the evening before by delivering a lecture on the art of fly fishing, underlining the importance of getting into the water without causing a ripple. Suzie hung on his every word.

James and I were in high spirits returning to the hotel next evening; between us we had caught three salmon. There was already a fish on the slab in the hall, a nice, fresh 10 pounder. We took the key to the rod-room and, on opening the door, were greeted with the familiar sight of Suzie's waders hanging upside down and dripping all over the floor.

"Dear God," said James. "She's fallen in again. Poor old Guy, he must have had a dreadful day."

He had. "Quite unspeakably dreadful," he said. He had decided that morning on setting out to be philosophical about the whole project and to endure stoically what the day might bring. It was to take his considerable reserves of chivalry. He said, with a shudder, that he would draw a veil over most of the day, all the blunderings and entanglements, the hooking of a sheep which was minding its own business on the bank. From Suzie herself we learned that the sheep had taken exception to this and had fled into the field. When she followed, at full speed, her reel screeching, she had started a stampede among the flock. As far as she was concerned it had been a very minor incident; the fly had ultimately come free, accompanied by a large chunk of wool, and neither she nor the ewe were any the worse for the gallop across the water meadows. It had seemed to upset Guy, though.

It had been Guy's intention to get Suzie back to the hotel in the afternoon on the pretext of packing for the journey home the next morning. He then planned to sneak back to the river for two or three hours' peaceful fishing, having done his duty manfully. It was not to be.

Suzie wanted to try again in a rather nice pool where she had seen a salmon jump earlier in the day. There was a 6 ft bank, but once in the water, wading on the shingle bottom was easy. She announced that she was going to get into the river quietly if it killed her, and with exaggerated stealth she edged down the bank. Guy was taking no chances with the rod and was holding it for her until she was safely in the water, which was just as well since her entry was not quite what she had intended. She slipped and fell in with a great splash.

Suzie was mortified. She got to her feet, rising from the water like a well-fed hippo, and demanded her rod. "I'm in, and I'm wet, and I'm damn-well going to fish while I'm here."

Guy handed her the rod, unable to utter any word of sympathy. He said he was going downstream to the next pool, and he strode off, furious. He had not gone very far when there was a loud scream from upstream. For one glorious moment he thought she must be drowning. Reluctantly he turned back.

Suzie had hooked a salmon with her third cast. Guy could not bear to relate her playing of it. "Suffice it to say that the whole performance was unorthodox and extremely noisy," he said.

A first ever salmon is usually toasted with champagne, and we saluted the fish and Suzie in some style. She was understandably exultant, and after drinking about a bottle of champagne was sufficiently uninhibited to expound her views on fishing. She had, she said, always thought this nonsense of creeping about quite unnecessary. Not only did salmon not mind a bit of splashing, it seemed likely that it actually attracted them; they came to see what was going on. What a pity, she said, that it was the last day, because she was eager to try out her theory. But never mind, she was greatly looking forward to coming with us on our next fishing trip.

Rocky

It was hot. For April it was extraordinarily hot, and bright - quite the wrong conditions required for salmon fishing. All day the sun had beaten down, at first burning dew off the fields, then making our waders hot to the touch. My Barbour jacket weighed heavily, but there were, as there always are, so many essentials filed away in its pockets that it was easier to wear it than to have to find somewhere to put fly-boxes, priest, string and all the necessary impedimenta.

We fished all day, up and down our beat, with no sign of a salmon; not a tug on the line, no sound of a splash, no sight of a silver side rolling in the water. Only little brown trout were rising to various hatches of flies in the shade of the trees on the bank.

By mid-afternoon I had had enough. James said he was going back up to Crocker's Pool to see if he could persuade a fish to take now that the sun was off that stretch of water. Was I coming? No, I was not. I was going to take my jacket off, jettison the net and sit down on the smooth white stones at Rocky Pool and commune with nature.

"If you do decide to cast in there," said James. "Remember that if you step off the shelf you will immediately find yourself in ten feet of water."

"I'm not going to fish any more," I said. "I'm just going to sit here until you get back."

James set off upstream for Crocker's. I sat. I watched the beautiful herd of cows in the field on the opposite bank; honey-coloured hides, great melting brown eyes, lazily grazing, tails swishing at flies. I watched a pair of mallard guarding their poorly concealed nest, and butterflies flitting thither and yon. I listened to a chaffinch singing his heart out on a branch above me. Wrens and robins were busy nesting, dippers were flying straight as arrows up and down the river. I watched a couple of buzzards quartering the dense woodland beyond the field.

Folding my jacket, I made a cushion for my head and I lay down on the hot stones. For a short time I drowsed. I could hear the river rippling, gurgling and splashing, and all was very peaceful.

I must have slept for a while, because I was rudely awakened by a cloud of midges and I realised that I was about to be eaten alive. Sitting up and looking around me, all was as before; James was nowhere to be seen.

Slowly I got to my feet. The river looked very inviting and I waded into the water. Now, if you are going to stand in the river there is no point in not having a rod in your hand, and if you have a rod, why not cast?

I let out line and slowly worked my way down the pool. Nothing. But I wasn't expecting to connect with a fish anyway, I was just filling in time and not really concentrating.

There was still no sign of James, so I went to the top of the pool and started down again. About the third cast the line stopped and, thinking that my fly had caught on the rock shelf, I gave a gentle tug to free it. The 'snag' moved, not with any great excitement, but it swam smoothly away upstream.

My predicament was obvious. I had left the net on the bank with my jacket. My waders were rolled down to below my knees and I was not able to roll them up again, my hands being otherwise occupied. Perhaps I should also mention that I had never before played a salmon entirely on my own. I had hooked fish when I had been alone, but James, never far away, had always come at a hand-gallop, arriving in time to apply net or tailer.

I called just once "James," but he was a mile upstream and I was absolutely alone with the fish.

At first I thought it was going to be easy; the salmon was quietly swimming about and I was on a nice easy shingle bank, but then he realised that all was not as it should be and he tried to rid himself of the fly. He jumped and dived, making for the big shelf, where I knew he would cut the nylon cast against the sharp rocks.

Faced with the alternatives of losing the fish or getting wet feet, there seemed very little real choice and I waded in as far as I dared on the shelf, keeping the line as high as possible. After about twenty minutes he was getting tired and started to roll on the surface, which was just as well since my heart was racing and my arm ached.

I started to walk slowly backwards toward the shingle beach and, to my surprise, the fish followed me quietly into the shallows. Five yards from the shore he turned on his side in some eighteen inches of water. I was afraid to pull him in any further in case the hook came out, so I managed to find a handkerchief in my pocket, wrapped it round my hand, grasped him firmly just above the tail and towed him up the shingle towards my jacket and the priest. He flapped a bit but I hung on grimly.

We arrived safely, well away from the water's edge and I delivered the last rites with a sigh of relief.

I had just emptied my waders and wrung out my sodden socks, when James appeared on the horizon. I had time to conceal the fish in the net under a bush before going to meet him.

"Anything in Crocker's?" I asked.

"No, nothing. Much too hot. They are probably all having a siesta. We might as well make our way home."

He came down the bank to pick up the lunch bag, my jacket and the net, when he caught sight of the fish. His face was a study.

"Good lord, you've got a salmon. Clever girl. How did you manage that? Where did you get it? What time? How long did it take you? What fly?"

"I took him at the head of the pool. He gave me a bit of trouble - tried to get under the shelf, but I waded well out and when he was tired I beached him on the shingle."

A single salmon on the slab of a fishing pub is rather like a hole-in-one at golf in that the lucky person is obliged to buy drinks all round. It was with the greatest possible pleasure that I bought the wine for dinner that night.

A proper Big Fish

By the tine I had soaked off the mud and fatigue of the day and had made my way downstairs, the bar of the fishing pub was full. James was deep in conversation with one of the locals, a weather beaten old farmer.

"I was standing on the bridge below your water today," said the old Devonian. "And there was a proper big fish making his way uptream. Should be in one of your lower pools by morning."

Devonians are nice, hard-working, honest people and I would not want to suggest that they are economical with the truth, but fishernen who haven't seen sight of their quarry for a couple of days tend to be a bit gullible, and hotel landlords and local anglers, being kind, like to give disappointed visitors some encouragement.

James made all the right noises, thanked the man profusely for this valuable information and bought him another drink before we parted company and went in to dinner.

A party of us, usually eight or nine in number, always took the pub and its fishing for ten days in early April. Over dinner we all compared notes: the river was high and slightly coloured and there had been no sight or sound of fish. It was also bitterly cold, with sleet showers, which made the river banks slippery and the long day out of doors extremely tiring.

"I wonder if he really saw a fish?" I asked James.

"I'd take that with a large pinch of salt, but at least the water is falling and fining down now. It certainly looks more hopeful than when we arrived."

The lowest beat of the 'Angler's Rest' water was a long walk from the fishing hut, and its banks were so exposed to an east wind that few people thought it worth the trouble in inclement weather. There were two pools; the upper pool was fed by a good run in over a stickle and it had an easy shingle beach, ideal for wading. The lower pool was extremely difficult. It was possible, with care, to wade down the pool, but having reached the botton it was necessary to climb up a tree with its roots in the water to reach dry land again. There was no way of retracing one's steps, the weight and flow of the water was such that it was very much one way only. The tree marked the boundary between our water and the adjacent private fishing. All in all, this was for advanced and agile students only.

James put me in at the easier upper pool while he, in breast waders, began to fish the lower pool.

I happened to glance downstream between casts and was immediately aware that James was standing with the water lapping perilously near his armpits, and also that he had stopped fishing and was changing his fly, the butt of his rod and the reel tucked safely down the top of his waders.

I got out of the river and crept along the bank to see what was happening.

"Keep down," he whispered. "I've just had a salmon follow me. I'm going to change to a Thunder and Lightning; perhaps he will take that.

I sat on the bank, well off the skyline, while James cast across the pool with the new fly. Suddenly his rod-tip bent, he gave a great cry and the fish was on.

For some twenty minutes the salmon rushed up and down. It least into the air, leaving us breathless with excitement; it then plunged to the bottom of the pool, where it spent ten minutes nose down in the deep channel in the middle of the river, and refused to move at all.

I could see James applying side-strain as hard as he dared and, at last, the fish surfaced again. When it rolled on its side we could see that it was, indeed, a large fish.

James, now with waders full of water, followed it downstream. He called to me to say that the fish was about beaten and would I please come in and tail it for him.

The water was icy. I was wearing only thigh waders and almost immediately I was in the river up to my waist. Too late I realised that I would have been better to have taken my waders and one pair of socks off altogether.

We followed the fish down the river, looking for some backwater out of the current. By this time we were well below the tree and out of our own water, some two hundred yards from where the fish had been hooked.

At some point an elderly gentleman had appeared on the bank to fish, but we had been so busy that we had not noticed his arrival. He waited quietly until, at last, the salmon was safely tailed and then he sprang into action.

First of all I passed him the rod, then he pulled me out of the river. James, having dispatched the fish with his priest and having threaded a piece of stout string through its gills so that there was no way he could lose it, was persuaded to part with his precious catch.

All this done, the Good Samaritan poured me a generous slug of brandy from his flask and we stood admiring the fish while I gulped the fiery liquid gratefully.

"What about me then?" cried an indignant husband, still up to his chest in the river.

We heaved him up the bank and handed him the flask.

"Lovely fish, about twenty pounds I should say," said our rescuer. "What fly did he take?"

"A Thunder and Lightning, one of my own tie with plenty of jay hackle," said James. "Here, I've got several, perhaps you would like a couple; it might prove to be the fly of the day."

A combination of brandy and euphoria at having landed the salmon in rather difficult circumstances had taken our minds off one small problem. To get back on to our own beat we had to get into the water again in order to climb up the tree, because the boundary was also marked by an impenetrable bramble hedge and barbed wire.

Once past all the obstacles we were faced with the task of emptying our waders, a matter of lying down and sticking our legs in the air. I was just about to roll my waders down with a view to removing them, when James shouted for me to stop.

"Stop. Don't take them off or you'll never get them on again."

He explained that we had to find a suitable slope, then we had to decide whether we wanted the water down our fronts or backs. We were wet enough already, but our cries were pitiful as we lay with cold river water sluicing over us.

James found a small but thick branch, to which he tied the salmon, and we started the long jog-trot back to the fishing hut, carrying the burden between us.

We were very late for lunch and the other members of our party were wondering what had happened to us. We arrived, blue with cold and very wet and muddy, carrying salmo salar. Our friends fed us hot soup and more brandy, and Tinker insisted on driving us back to the hotel to dry out.

It was unknown for us ever to arrive back to the 'Angler's Rest' in the middle of a fishing day and the landlord and his wife came out, anxious to see what was wrong. When they saw the state we were in mud to the ears and shivering uncontrollably with cold - they took the fish from us and rushed to run us hot baths. The landlord poured us schooners of sherry, and, in truth, we were in more danger of drowning in our baths than we had ever been in the river.

The salmon weighed in at 22 pounds.

I spent the afternoon in bed with a hot water bottle. James borrowed some dry waders, put on warm clothes and went back to the river. He said he didn't feel the cold at all, in fact his feet didn't touch the bottom; he seemed to be floating. He did catch another very much smaller salmon from an easy place near the pub, but he was very hazy about the exact details.

Our friend, the farmer, was in the bar again that evening, having heard that a good fish had been caught on our lower beat. Bush telegraph is very efficient up and down Devon rivers.

"Ar, you 'ad 'im then," he said with immense satisfaction.

"I told 'ee he were a proper big fish."

He needed no persuasion to join us in wetting the salmon's head.

"I was crossing the little bridge this evening," he said, fixing James with his wise old eyes set in a leathery face. He paused for effect. "Saw a couple of proper big fish running up. Should be in one of your middle pools come morning."

The one that got away

A Very Old Friend has exercised his right to offer some 'constructive criticism'.

"I've read your fishing stories," he said. "They're not bad, but they're just too neat. You always come home with a nice basket of trout, or you catch a salmon, or James does. No matter what happens you always manage to triumph."

Somewhat aggrieved, I said "They're all absolutely true."

"I dare say. Anyone who has ever fished with you and James will admit that you are both incident-prone. But don't you ever come home empty-handed?"

I said of course we had blank days, but they were too boring to write about. No-one wanted to read about failure.

"Nonsense," he said. "If it wasn't for the ones that get away most fishermen would have nothing to talk about."

So I decided to tell him the saga of the monster salmon.

Many years ago, long before we met, James shared a beat with two friends on the middle Torridge. Salmon fishing was vastly different in those pre-pollution and pre-UDN days and James says it was not unusual for him to take a dozen salmon in a week when conditions were right.

He had a friend who owned first-class water several miles downstream, a widely acknowledged expert with whom he often fished. About the end of April, 1953, this friend hooked a salmon in high water. He knew at once it was a heavy fish and when it jumped the sight was breathtaking. Telling James later, he said it was much the biggest fish he had ever seen, not only in that river but anywhere else for that matter, and he estimated it to be well over 40 pounds. After that initial jump the fish and he settled down to a dour, deep struggle. for half-an-hour or so nothing very dramatic happened; the fish cruised majestically up and down the pool, but James' friend was not too anxious since he had 18 pound nylon line with a Devon Reflex minnow. However, suddenly he 'felt something go' and realised that one point of his treble hook must either have broken or come away. To his relief the fish remained solidly hooked and for the next twenty minutes the status quo was maintained, the fish swimming slowly and deep out in mid-stream, with James' friend keeping up as much strain as he dared. Then, to his dismay, he 'felt something else go' and knew that the end was inevitable, that he must be down to his last prong. Finally, ten minutes later, the fish was lost. Reeling in, he found that all three arms of the triangle had broken off at the bend, which surprised him since he always used heavy Martin outpoint triangles and had never before known one to break.

The next part of my story is well documented, appearing as it does in the late L.R.N. Gray's book 'Torridge Fishery', published in 1957.

In May, 1953, Gray was fishing his bottom beat, several miles upstream of James' friend's water, and, whilst landing a small salmon on a fly, he saw the monster rise. He wrote 'I doubted my eyesight the first time I saw him, but he came right out . . and I put him down at well over 40 pounds - probably nearer 50 pounds'.

Very excited, Gray changed to a strong spinning rod with a multiplying reel and a heavy line. He cast out a 'Land 'em Loach' on a 20 pound trace, the great fish took it immediately and a desperate struggle ensued. After a most strenuous half-hour, during which time Gray had to wade out into the river up to his neck to follow the fish up and downstream, it ran under the bank and cut the trace on a root-stub, which would have been above water at normal height. Gray was too heartbroken to do anything but moan and sag into a wet heap on the bank. All the skin was gone from both thumbs and he was thoroughly soaked 'with all desire to fish out the rest of the day quite gone', and all he could do was to trail home.

He had heard that a huge fish had been hooked and lost downstream, but he heard no more of the monster.

Towards the end of May that year, James visited Devon for a week to fish his beat, some three miles above Gray's water. He stayed at a fishing lodge on the river nearby and his old friend, the bailiff, hearing of his arrival, sought him out. He told him that the local postman, on his early morning round, had seen a most enormous salmon jump in Bridge Pool at the top of James' beat, and had described it as being 'as big as his motor bicycle'.

That night it rained up on the moor and the river rose and coloured. A morning's fishing produced nothing, but the water was beginning to drop and clear. Immediately after lunch James resumed fishing Bridge Pool, spinning with an 8 ft cane rod, 20 pound nylon and a Devon Reflex minnow.

At exactly 1.40 p.m. (he always looks at his watch when he hooks a fish) he was taken by a large salmon. After some manoeuvring the fish set off downstream, out of the pool, closely followed by James. There were no immediate obstacles but, some 50 yards below, a row of bushes lined the bank. Normally the river was not too deep there and could be negotiated safely in chest waders, but not at that height of water. The fish continued downstream into a long canal like stretch and, as James' line left his reel, he was aware that the 150 yards of nylon must be perilously near exhaustion. By this time he had collected an audience of two twelve year old boys and, since they obviously knew about fishing and were eager to help him, he discarded his waders and clothing. This was not the easiest of operations, even with the aid of the boys, to whom he was forced to entrust the rod for very brief moments, but once down to underpants and socks, he took to the water, carrying his rod aloft, and was able to get below the bushes and regain the bank. Using a pullover as a towel, he dried himself as best he could with one hand and re-dressed in shirt, trousers and jacket. One boy was dispatched to the lodge a quarter of a mile away with instructions to bring him shoes and socks, whilst James proceeded to give the salmon his full attention once more.

The river was deep and sluggish, the bank high and sheer. About 15 yards from the top of the stretch an old oak tree stump, some 12 ft high, leaned out from the bank into the river, and there was no way round it. The boy arrived back with the shoes and socks, accompanied by the manager of the lodge, not himself a fisherman. Making use of the 20 yards or so available to him, James managed to walk the fish up until it was opposite him. Although the bank was so steep, at one point a small bush grew from it about half way down, and James persuaded the manager, assisted by the boys, to lower himself down until he perched on the bush, gaff in hand.

James had a swivel 2 ft above his bait and the plan, as outlined to the reluctant manager, was that he would attempt to bring the fish near to the bank; then he would try to get it near to the surface.

When the swivel appeared out of the water it meant that the fish, although not visible, was 2 ft below it and was to be gaffed firmly, taking care not to cut the nylon. If he succeeded, he was to hang on for dear life as the fish would be displeased and would kick hard.

After ten minutes of careful and skillful playing, first the nylon and then the swivel broke surface. James and the two boys were in a state of high excitement and cried 'Now! Now! Take him! Now! '

For a moment the fish's back appeared on the surface, about the size of a full-grown, well-nourished pig. The manager's nerve broke. "It's too big," he shouted. "It'll pull me in. I'll drown."

He proceeded to scramble back up the bank. Unable to face the reproaches of the boys and James' obvious disgust, he declared that he must return to the lodge to prepare tea for his guests, and departed.

The fish had been on for about two hours.

For what seemed like an age James and the fish were hopelessly deadlocked, the salmon having resumed his deep, slow cruising in mid-stream. Help and support then arrived in the form of another angler who had been fishing the lodge water. He was a much more determined character than the manager and suggested that, as his rod was 10 ft long, he might be able to lift James' line over the tree stump - giving him another 50 yards of bank from which to work. He fixed a twig to the top ring of his rod; James' line was placed in the cleft thus formed and, with the aid of the tallest boy and after several abortive attempts, it was lifted over the stump. James was now much better placed.

The great fish stayed well out in the middle of the river, drifting slowly downstream with the current. On reaching the shallower end of the stretch it would check and settle on the bottom, then James walked it laboriously upstream again, the rod bent and the 20 pound nylon so taut it seemed to hum in the light breeze. At the top of the stretch James would move down rapidly opposite the fish and apply all the side-strain he could muster in an attempt to bring it closer. Quite often he got the fish within a yard or two of the bank, but it would turn, make for the middle of the river and go downstream again. Of the two it seemed more likely that James was going to be the first to tire.

By 5p.m. the situation was essentially unchanged, except that a small group of spectators had assembled. The angler had remained loyally at James' side, giving encouragement and advice.

"Sooner or later you'll be able to get him into the bank and up to the surface," he said with enviable optimism. "He must be well hooked and you've got strong nylon. I've got an idea about gaffing him. Wait here, I'll be gone about twenty minutes. Just hang on."

Taking the boys with him, the angler disappeared at a smart trot. When he returned he had brought with him a coil of stout rope, a spade and more people.

"Plenty of help here to hold me," he said. "They can let me down the bank slowly and I'll cut steps as I go. When I get down to the water I'll cut a good foothold and then you can try to bring him to me. If I can gaff him they'll haul me up quickly."

This plan was put into effect; the angler was lowered down the bank, cutting a series of rather insecure footholds as he went. Several times he slipped, and if it had not been for the rope he would have joined the fish in the river.

At last he pronounced himself ready, and passed the spade up to an assistant on the bank. He extended his gaff and said to James "It's up to you now. I'm set. If you can bring him near enough and get the swivel out of the water I'll gaff him, even if he weighs a ton."

Anxiously watched by the onlookers, James gradually brought the salmon closer and closer. He got it to within four or five yards of the waiting gaff when there was a great shout from the bank and spectators were pointing upstream in horror.

"Look! Look what's coming down."

There, at the top of the stretch, loosened by the recent flood, a sizeable tree trunk, well endowed with spiky branches, was bobbing its way downstream. James re-doubled his efforts, but there was absolutely nothing he could do. Inexorably the tree bore down on the line, entangling it in its branches, and then it swept on down the river. The reel screeched; there was a loud snap and only a loose end of nylon came back.

It was exactly 6p.m.

The intrepid angler was hauled up the bank. No-one spoke, but one of the boys wept openly. James says he was so overwhelmed with fatigue that he was completely numb and could only stand there, looking at the broken line.

The intrepid angler took his arm and, turning to the crowd, made the only possible suggestion in the circumstances.

"Let's make for the nearest bar," he said. "I think we all need a drink."

My Very Old Friend appeared terribly upset by this tale of woe, even though it happened so many years ago, when James and the world were young.

"How perfectly dreadful," he said. "Poor James. You can't possibly write about that. Far too depressing. That's the saddest fishing story I've ever heard."

"Quite," I said with some satisfaction.

"Was the fish ever seen again?"

"As far as we know it was never seen alive again. But, interestingly enough, the following spring James had a letter from his friend, the bailiff, saying that his colleague who looked after the upper reaches of the Torridge had come across the body of a dead cock kelt which was so large, even in its decayed state, that he got it out of the river and weighed it. It was 38 pounds. James likes to think that at least the great fish fulfiled its destiny."

Trouble with waders

I may appear lackadaislcal about fishing tackle, but the reverse is true of my husband. In that mental tundra between January and March - no shooting, no fishing, no golf - he prepares for the coming season. There is an orgy of fly-tying, from tubes for salmon to the tiniest dry patterns. Reels, already cleaned and oiled, are inspected. Rods are checked and spigots rubbed with candle-grease. Nets and tailers are examined. Pockets of jackets and waistcoats are replenished with essentials. Spinning baits are sorted and triangles replaced. Lists are made. Nothing is left to chance.

Over the years there have been two main sources of discomfort while fishing for salmo salar in what we are pleased to call an English spring. One is gloves. I have complained bitterly about frozen, wet hands when the rest of me has been dry, encased in waxed cotton and rubber. Recently, looking through one of his favourite catalogues, James announced that he had found just the thing: "Guaranteed waterproof and warm. Perfect."

On arrival the mitts seemed all that had been claimed for them. Of black water-resistant material, they were comfortable and came well up over the wrists. James did raise one small doubt: 'They're fine, but a bit slippery. I wouldn't like to have to hand-tail a fish wearing them.'

However, waders present much the greatest difficulty. My studded thigh waders are no trouble at all, but James is unhappy unless he is in a river up to his armpits. He has a splendid pair of chest waders in some thick green material, bought from Hardy's for a king's ransom. They are warm, waterproof, resistant to barbed wire and probably to shot; they will last a lifetime, but unfortunately their weight is commensurate with their strength. I can hardly lift them and James has difficulty in walking in them, although once in the water they are superb. A series of lightweight stocking waders have punctured at the sight of brambles and perished no matter how carefully stored. The necessary overboots are the devil to get on and off.

The same catalogue offered black rubberized chest waders light, flexible and durable. Manufactured abroad, there was some delay in delivery, and it was finally arranged that they be sent direct to the fishing pub to await our arrival.

Sure enough, the parcel was waiting as promised. But James failed to appreciate the merriment of the rest of the party in the rod-room the following morning. The new waders were slightly tacky so that it required a great deal of talcum powder to get him poured into them. His tailor describes him as a 'tall, slim fit', and when he stood up it was obvious that the waders had been made for a man with short legs and an enormous girth. Their leg's ended well below his hips and, at chest level, they sagged in a pouch which would have delighted a kangaroo with quintuplets.

The only alternative was the Hardy 'heavies', and since our beat for the day involved walking over two large fields, James decided to make do with the new waders. By crossing the braces, pleating the bulge and tucking it inside his jacket he managed, but his usual athletic stride was reduced to a hobble. In the water the waders made fishing difficult, but not impossible. The pouch escaped from time to time and had to be tucked back under his jacket, but he reached the bottom of Long Pool without incident.

At the end of Long Pool it is just possible in chest waders to fish a further twenty paces under the trees and then get out of the water using a convenient tree stump. He had just reached the stump when a fish took him.

Knowing that he was in an awkward place with no room to manoeuvre, I went down to the bottom of the pool and waited with my net. The fish ran downstream and had to be coaxed back several times, and when James finally walked it up into the main pool it was about beaten. At full stretch on the bank, I still could not quite reach with my net and he steered the salmon gently towards me.

Just as it came within range there was an anguished cry as the hook came away. The next few seconds seemed to pass in slow motion. James threw his rod at me crying 'Take', and leant forward to tail the fish by hand. How right he had been about the mitts. First he picked the exhausted salmon up just above the tail with his right hand, but it promptly slipped from his grasp. Then he grabbed it with both hands round the middle and clutched it to his chest, where it again shot from his embrace, like a pip from an orange, and disappeared into the top of his waders, the pouch having come free as he bent forward. With the additional weight of the salmon the great pouch sank under water and the waders filled.

I had never before seen a man with an irate 91lb salmon inside his waders. Most interesting, as was his commentary on the situation while he scrambled ashore, holding up the front of the pouch with both hands to prevent the fishe's escape. Climbing up the steep bank, hands fully occupied but pushed from the rear by his faithful wife, was even more difficult. For the first time I fully understood Sisyphus's problem. Eventually we reached a flat, safe place, where he lay down so that water and salmon were disgorged and last rites were finally administered.

Removing the boots took some time and the waders had to be rolled off, but eventually, having replaced the boots, we were ready to make across the fields to the car, James talking longingly of a hot bath and something alcoholic to ward off pneumonia. We happened to be travelling in my new station wagon, so it can be readily understood why I refused to let him sit in the front on my pristine upholstery. It was the final indignity to arrive back to the hotel very wet, smelling strongly of fish and sittlng in what in effect was the boot.

For the rest of our stay the Hardy 'heavies' were pressed into service.

I am told the gloves are excellent for shooting; they are certainly perfect for rowing a boat in cold weather, but picking up a live salmon with them is not recommended.

The waders are hanging in our garage. We are looking for an angler, male or female, with large feet, very short legs and an approximate girth of 60 inches.

The Posthumous Salmon

George Scobie's favourite place was the tail of Oak Pool in the summer dusk. There, as the light faded and bats began to fly, sea trout dropped back into the shallower water.

As a young man he had often fished there all night, revelling in the soft velvet darkness, where the only sounds were the breeze stirring the great trees on the opposite bank and the rustlings of small night creatures.

George had fished all over the world, but he maintained that Oak pool at night had a magic of its own; that it was the only place where he became truly one with the river.

We met him on our first visit to the 'Anglers Rest'. He took time and trouble to show us the pools and places where fish might lie. He made us free of a lifetime's lore, and after that we saw him regularly, often arranging our visits to the river to co-incide with his.

Never large, as the years passed George seemed to shrink until, when he was 80 summers young, he was like a dried leaf. He attributed this to all the sun, wind and rain to which he had been exposed in a lifetime's fishing.

Anglers tend to live long and do not generally fear death, seeing themselves as part of the natural order of things.

'When I go,' George would say, sipping a large whisky in the bar before dinner. "When I go I'd like to be in the tail of Oak Pool with a good sea-trout hooked."

George's sorties grew shorter and he moved with increasing difficulty as time went by, but he still loved to be driven down to Oak Pool on summer evenings. His particular friend, Tom, would drive him over the two fields and see him safely down the bank. George took every bit as much care as he always had, wading into position without a splash, and casting like the master he was. He never moved. I can remember him saying to me in my early sea-trout fishing days: 'No need to move about, my dear. Just stand still and the fish will come to you."

From time to time George would hook a fish, play it out, net it, dispatch it and stow it away in the waterproof bag he wore slung around his neck, without making a sound. He only ever fished with a single fly, which he rarely changed. If; occasionally, he was broken by a larger fish he would replace the whole cast, already tied up with a fly, which he kept wound round his hat. He could do this standing in the water, rod butt tucked into his waders, without making so much as a ripple. Tom, fishing just upstream, could tell when George had a fish only by the noise of his reel.

In the end an hour or so was about as long as he could manage, but he never came home empty-handed.

On one such evening they had returned to the hotel and were having a nightcap before retiring. George said, 'When I go, Tom, I'd like you to scatter my ashes at the tail of Oak Pool. I think I've had more sport there than anywhere else.'

Tom was a little taken aback, but as George seemed set on it he promised, but said he hoped it wouldn't be necessary quite yet.

George did not get his wish about where he would end his days. In fact, he caught a chill that same winter and died quietly in his own bed. Tom attended the funeral, and wondered how to approach George's widow about the ashes. He need not have worried, George had added a codicil to his will, and Mollie Scobie presented Tom with the small urn containing George and thanked him for carrying out her dear husband's last wish.

And so it was that on the first day of the spring salmon fishing, Tom was installed in the Angler's Rest. The river was high and coloured, and more rain was forecast. With the outlook so unpromising, Tom thought he had better go and fulfil his obligation without delay. After breakfast, armed with his spinning rod and with George's urn stowed safely in his poacher's pocket, Tom made his way straight to Oak Pool.

Once at the river a problem presented itself: there was a strong wind blowing from the opposite bank, and the usually accessible shingle was under 18 inches of rushing water. If he tried to scatter George the ashes would blow all over the place. If, on the other hand, he just threw the urn into the pool it might be carried off, possibly as far as the sea, which was not quite what had been intended.

Having considered the circumstances, Tom slid carefully down the grassy bank. With his rod in one hand, and supported by his wading staff, he made his way cautiously a few paces into the river.

He knew that in high water the tail of Oak Pool often held salmon and, a true fisherman, he thought he might as well have a few casts before disposing of George. He threw his one-ounce gold Toby well out into the swollen stream and brought it back slowly. On the third cast he hooked a fish.

During the ensuing struggle it was inevitable that Tom, wearing only thigh waders, should ship a considerable amount of water. However, eventually he coaxed the salmon within reach, tailed it and scrambled up the bank on his hands and knees, dragging his tailer and the flapping fish with him. Having administered the last rites he stood admiring his prize - a shining 17 pounder with sea lice.

Finally, Tom decided he had better get back to the hotel for dry clothes and a hot drink. He took off his waders and emptied them, then removed his jacket, the pockets of which were full of water. He was tipping it upside down when, to his horror, George's urn shot out of the poacher's pocket in a miniature waterfall. It bounced on the steep bank and splashed into the river. On impact the top flew off and George was scattered over the tail of Oak Pool. The urn was last seen bobbing downstream. George's wish had been fulfilled.

The landlord was delighted when Tom arrived back carrying his salmon - the first of the new season. 'Be sure to write it up in the book,' he said. 'I've prepared a new page for this year.'

Tom had a hot bath, put on dry clothes and ordered a large Scotch, with which he silently toasted his absent friend. There was a pristine page in the salmon book, all neatly ruled ready for the season's record. Tom entered the date, time, height of water, lure, weight of fish, and then paused at the remaining two columns. Under 'Name' he wrote: 'George Scobie', and under 'comments' he wrote 'Credit where credit is due'.

The downfall of Old Charlie

Old Charlie had been introduced into the chalk stream as a young two pounder some four years before. I would not go so far as to say that he had led a charmed life, for in his youth he had been hooked once and pricked several times.

On the occasion he took an artificial fly and found himself firmly attached to an angler's line, it could have happened to any trout, since it was Mayfly time. They had come thick and fast, first dancing through the air in the frenetic ballet of mating and then landing on the water like a carpet, drifting downstream, spent. In those circumstances fish dredge the flies rather than taking them individually and Charlie had, like many another, fallen prey to greed. However, the manner of his scooping the spent spinners from the surface meant that instead of being hooked neatly in the scissors, he had a barbless hook caught in the top of his mouth. It was enough to give him a fright, but not enough to bring him to the net. He had fought his way into a friendly patch of weed, shaken his head, and the hook had come free.

On two subsequent occasions he had been tempted by succulent looking upwinged duns, but sensing that there was something not quite right, a certain lifelessness, he had made only cautious passes at them, sufficient to make the angler on the bank exclaim that he had had a good trout on and off and to confirm Charlie's suspicion that things are not always what they seem. He was a good deal more careful after that.

In his second autumn in the chalk stream he had found himself a comely hen trout, who spawned in a small side-stream with a nice gravel bottom. Having played his part he had lost condition, since that sort of thing does tend to take it out off fish. However, the weight he had put on during the summer saw him through the winter.

The next season had been exceptional; food had been plentiful, with exuberant hatches of fly, plump larvae, beetles, water snails and sticklebacks, all in their seasons, and Charlie was not above consuming the fry of other trout when the opportunity arose.

He had fought for, and had won, a very desirable lie in the best pool on the chalk stream. He resided at the shallow end of this deep pool, his tail waving in the current of the outflow, his nose pointing into the deeper water. On the right bank there were bushes, which afforded shade, and on the left, from which the water was usually fished, there was long grass. There was just enough weed cover at both top and bottom of the pool to provide sanctuary when necessary. It would be difficult to imagine a more palatial home for a trout.

From his lie, Charlie could intercept any food travelling downstream, and he certainly did so, feeding with relish and growing ever more plump. The anglers who were privileged to fish those hallowed waters had no difficulty in presenting him with beautiful examples of the fly tyer's art, for it was easy enough to cast to him and they were all excellent men who could put a dry fly down on a sixpence. They all did their best, but he had become a most discerning trout. Probably the highest accolade anglers can bestow on their quarry is to give it a proper, familiar and affectionate name, which is how he came to be known as Old Charlie. He took absolutely no notice of anything they presented, and they tried everything - wonderfully lifelike flies which floated like thistledown - all of which he spurned. They used the finest nylon, and even occasionally tried him with an upstream nymph, but he lay in his chosen place, feeding on selected natural flies when there was a hatch and ignoring anything man-made with lofty disdain. If any angler was too persistent or cast badly and made the slightest splash, he would simply retreat deeper into the pool, as if to register cold disapproval of the intrusion.

However, every man jack of them, every time they passed that pool, felt that they should have a couple of casts over Old Charlie, more as a sort of greeting than anything, but always in the hope that one day he might decide to take. What a prize to boast about if they were to succeed, for they agreed among themselves that Old Charlie must weigh six pounds now, if he was an ounce.

In his fourth spring an eminent angler had been invited to fish the beat and, of course, he had been introduced to Old Charlie. Expert though he was, he had made no impression on the huge trout and his friends in the angling club had been secretly gratified that he, an acknowledged master, in spite of taking a good basket of fish on that fine May day had, like them, failed to fool their famous Charlie.

The angler returned again in September and asked the keeper as they walked along the bank together whether Old Charlie was still there. Yes, said the keeper, he was; bigger than ever, and it was high time someone caught him because, fine fish as he undoubtedly was, he was a snare and a delusion and was responsible for a good deal of wasted fishing time.

The expert had a few casts over Old Charlie's nose, but these offerings were treated with contempt, although the trout continued to feed on natural flies in a leisurely way. The expert wasted no more time, but reeled in and made his way downstream. He doubted that anyone would get the better of Old Charlie that season.

The expert was otherwise occupied all that September day, but, as he walked home upstream with the day's catch, he passed Old Charlie's lair and noticed that he was missing. Surely, he thought, no one had caught him in an unguarded moment; perhaps he had just gone down. However, as he watched, a massive rise against the far bank gave Old Charlie's position away. He had moved from his usual lie and was now stationed upstream, only a few yards from the bank and a couple of yards below a large bush which grew there, overhanging the river. He was certainly taking something from the surface, although a breeze had blown up and there was no visible hatch of fly. It was obvious that something very desirable was presenting itself to the trout; again and again he rose, gulped whatever it was from the surface and then retired to his new position against the bank.

The expert sat down, pondered and continued to observe. He finally noticed that the bush bore a fine crop of ripe, lush berries, dark purple in colour, almost black, and that from time to time in the slight breeze one would fall with a plop into the water, to be promptly engulfed by Old Charlie. The trout was not feeding on fly at all, he was busy consuming fruit.

The expert took out his box of dry flies and speculated for some time on what to choose. There was nothing there he fancied at all, nothing dark enough or big enough. He had, in the depths of his pocket, a small box of wet flies, which he had certainly not expected to use on this expedition, and from this he selected a large, buzzy Black and Peacock Spider, which he greased so that it would float. Very sneaky, he thought, but it might just do the trick. The cast also would have to go against all the tenets of a chalk stream; none of the usual setting down of the fly as softly as possible, a good PLOP was what was required.

The expert knelt down on the grass, had a couple of false casts and dropped the spider with a splash, just in front of Old Charlie's nose.

The trout was waiting for the arrival of the next berry and he darted forward eagerly, seizing the fly.

He very nearly escaped again, for as he came to the net the expert had it in mind to return him to his natural element. It was enough to have outwitted the trout, to have played him with skill, to have had the pleasure of the fight and the sight of such a glorious brown trout in the net. But, most unfortunately, Old Charlie had charged at the fly and had taken it right down his throat, so that when it was removed he bled profusely. Sorry as the expert was about this, he knew that if he returned him to the river he would probably die anyway, so he dispatched him as quickly as possible.

Old Charlie weighed 7 pounds.

There is always a sense of loss when such a fish is missing from his usual lie, and he was too revered to end up being eaten. The expert decided to have him mounted, with a suitable inscription, and to present him to the angling club.

Old Charlie looks very handsome in his glass case, with a plaque bearing his name, his weight and the date and place of his capture. The fly that was his downfall is not mentioned.

What are you doing down there?

We called it Sanctuary, although it had no official name. High, sheer banks on both sides were closely lined with great trees, their branches intermingling and hanging far out over the river. The very deep, slow-flowing water always held salmon, but that stretch - several hundred yards long - was absolutely inaccessible as far as fishing was concerned. It was quite impossible to cast a fly, or even to spin there.

One fine autumn day, as we walked past from a lower beat, James remarked that if there were even a small gap in the trees it would be possible to throw a spinner into the river below. I agreed, but gave it no further thought.

Next spring we arrived in the evening for a week's salmon fishing. We met the bailiff in the bar and, as usual, he gave us news of the past winter. Apparently a gale had brought down one of the largest trees, and it had fallen straight across Sanctuary, partially blocking the river. The River Board, well equipped to deal with such emergencies, was notified immediately. Fortunately that area of bank was easily reached from the road across dry grazing land. The huge tree was hauled out, cut up and disposed of. The bailiff said the whole operation had been neat and quick and no harm had been done.

In the morning we were out early, eager to get to the river. The water was not particularly high, but still a little coloured from a recent spate. James was fishing a sunk tube fly, and I opted for a No 4 silver Mepps.

We fished a couple of pools together, then parted company. I said I would walk downstream. 'Right,' James said. 'I'll go over this pool again, and then follow you. I won't be long, unless anything happens.'

As I walked past Sanctuary the change was obvious. There was a gap of some 20 paces where the tree had been. Standing there I noticed, about 10 ft below me, a small shelf, just above the water, with a bush at one end. At that moment a salmon rose just downstream of the shelf.

Without thinking, I unhooked my spinner and cast it across, just above where the fish had shown. As it came round it was taken, and the fight was on.

Don't ask me how I got down the bank, I simply do not remember. Judging from the amount of mud on my back I must have glissaded, but all I can say with confidence is that one minute I was standing on the high bank and the next I was perched precariously on a small ledge with a fish hooked. The tailer was still on its string round my back, although I found later it had inflicted a spectacular bruise in my excursion down the bank. Luckily the salmon was not large and was reasonably obliging in that there were no gymnastics and it didn't run far. I was in no position to follow it anywhere.

Eventually, played right out and lying on its side in the water at my feet, I managed to tail it and get it on to the shelf. The rod butt was stuffed down one wader, and I wedged the tailer in the bush while the coup de grâce was delivered. Not until the fish was dead and I had tied a loop of string through its gills and secured it to the bush did I feel it was safe. At least now if I fell in the fish would not be lost.

Lowering myself cautiously, so that I was sitting on the shelf with my feet dangling in the water, I got a good grip on the bush and waited for assistance. one thing was certain - James was not going to be best pleased to find me in such a predicament.

The whole incident had taken at least 30 minutes, and I hadn't long to wait before James came along. I called out; he heard me, but couldn't immediately make out where I was. when he finally looked over the bank and saw me he said, 'What on earth are you doing down there?' Then he saw the salmon and realisation dawned. I must say he established that I was unhurt before getting cross: 'You might have broken an ankle, or your neck,' he said. 'What a stupid thing to do.'

'Yes,' I said, contrite. 'I know. I'm sorry. Can you help me up please.'

Telling me to stay absolutely still and on no account to let go of the bush - as if I had any intention of doing so - he set off for the hut to get some rope, muttering about wasting good fishing time. Fortunately our old friend, the farmer, was in a nearby field with his jeep. He drove James to the hut and then brought him back. They both came and peered down at me.

'Beats me how Mrs Armstrong got down there,' the farmer said cheerfully. 'But she'll be easier to get up than a bullock or a sheep. At least we won't have to climb down and tie the rope round her.'

He seemed to relish the prospect of the rescue. The rope was lowered, and the salmon was sent up first. James then tied a loop so that I could put both arms through it in case I slipped. Relinquishing my hold on the friendly bush I stood up and was able to hand my rod to the farmer, who was lying on his stomach on the bank to receive it. Finally they hauled me up the sheer face. I started well enough, leaning away from the perpendicular in true mountaineering style, but without the advantage of crampons or an ice axe my feet slipped and I bounced against the muddy bank as they drew me up.

The farmer took us back to the hut in his jeep, where we presented him with the 8 lb salmon and thanked him for his help.

James tried to make me promise never to do anything like that again, and I did go so far as to say I would be more careful in future. But forswear all recklessness for ever? Certainly not. If a salmon rises as an angler passes, be the access easy, difficult, or even well nigh impossible, then the mind leaves the body and the cast is made with no thought of the consequences.

Runaway boat

Those were the days, when I sat on a cushion in the stern of the boat, watching the water go by. Emma stood, paws on the thwart, head held high, sniffing the breeze. She and I would observe the day from our positions of ease; the mountains that swept down to the road that wound past the lake, sheep on the hillsides, a shepherd working his dogs. I would comment on fish rising and how beautiful it all was, while James toiled at the oars, pulling with steady, powerful strokes. Halcyon days. We have some old fishing prints showing much the same sort of thing: elegant ladies with parasols recline in punts while the men impress them with their prowess at the poles.

I can remember the day which marked the end of this idyll and ensured for all time that the boat was my responsibility. Some valleys have moderate slopes, carved as by a gentle hand, sheltered, peaceful, undisturbed. Our Welsh valley had the appearance of a mighty hand having delivered a karate chop to the mountains. At each end there was a narrow cleft through which the wind could blow, funnelled, often accompanied by driving rain. The lake, large, long, and deep, filled the valley.

We had drifted quietly against the lee shore at the far end when a squall blew up quite suddenly. We sat with collars up, waiting for it to blow itself out; Emma sulked in the bottom of the boat, making soulful eyes at us as if we were to blame for her discomfort. Once the worst was past we expected the promised clear skies to emerge, but they did not; instead, the wind remained steady about half way up the Beaufort scale.

I suppose we could have left the boat and, carrying our rods, bags and fish, could have walked the mile or so back against the blast to the comfort of the hotel. But James is a great one for finishing anything he starts and it was a point of honour to get the boat back to the jetty. He suggested that if we each took an oar and pulled hard we would be able to make it back with our reputations intact, while everyone else had abandoned ship and run for cover.

Anyone who has ever pulled a single oar will be able to predict what happened next. We went round in circles, James hurling instructions to the 'crew' which fell well short of his usual sweet-natured suggestions. I pulled as hard as I could, getting crosser and crosser; Emma growled softly, thoroughly disgruntled in the rising bilge.

Our progress, if it can be called that, was watched with amused interest by all who had given up the struggle and had left their boats beached for later retrieval. They observed our efforts from the warmth and comfort of the bar, whose windows overlooked the lake, and one unprincipled angler actually took bets on the state of the marriage if and when we finally made it to safety. We crept painfully slowly along the shore, trying to keep out of the worst of the wind, zig zagging uncontrollably, sometimes bumping against the bank and sometimes drifting out into the lake and the white water, but eventually we arrived - the only boat to have made it home.

Later I received a lecture on rowing. It was, said James, not so much a matter of strength - witness a friend of ours who could row up the lake like the wind, and she was no more muscular than I, although it was true that she had been brought up and had learned to row on the Menai Straight - it was more a matter of timing. We should, he suggested kindly, try again in better conditions. We did, and our wake suggested a giant serpent with colic, this time because in my efforts to prove that I was not as feeble as he thought I pulled far too hard and in jerks. I remember that we exchanged some rather harsh words in the course of that erratic excursion down the lake, and in the heat of the moment I made a fatal mistake.

"I would do better on my own," I said, and I have paid dearly for that utterance ever since. Taking both oars I propelled us relatively straight to our destination.

That lake in Wales was, in those days, full of wild brown trout, not large but extremely lively. It also had an autumn run of salmon and sea trout which made their way up a small tributary from the main river. These fish eventually spawned in the clear, gravel-bottomed feeder streams fed by mountain rainwater, but it was very difficult to tell where they might lie in the lake itself. In the evenings they could sometimes be seen splashing off the reed beds, but very rarely could be persuaded to take there. Occasionally, fishing with a size 14 Mallard and Claret for trout from a promontory on the bank, it would suddenly take off with a great screech of the reel before the fine nylon broke.

However, there were certain places where a salmon might be expected to lie - especially first thing in the morning before boat traffic disturbed the peace of the lake and they dispersed to unknown lairs in the depths. Immediately after breakfast we would row quietly into position and drift down towards the stream. We had been rewarded for this sort of stealth on several occasions. The salmon were not large, anything from 5 to 9 pounds, and we had a system. If I hooked one, James would control the boat while it was played and he would then net it for me. But if he hooked a fish I would row gently ashore so that he could play it from the bank since I, being small, had difficulty in netting a salmon from the boat.

On the morning in question I had on a No 8 Peter Ross, which was taken with enthusiasm by a fresh 5 pounder. It was landed within fifteen minutes, James having eased the boat well away from the bank so as not to disturb any others that might be gathered at the mouth of the stream. We made a large semicircle and drifted slowly down to the same place, and this time James hooked a salmon of similar size on a Stoat's Tail.

All went according to plan: I manoeuvred the boat away from the taking place and beached it, while James climbed ashore and continued to play his fish from the bank. We were extremely pleased with ourselves; it was not yet 9.30 and we had outwitted not only the salmon but all the other lazier anglers who had lingered at the breakfast table. But 'Pride goeth before destruction and an haughty spirit before a fall'. It was Emma who tried to warn us that all was not as it should be.

"Quiet, Emma," said James, as he extracted the fly with some difficulty because it was well embedded in the scissors. I was watching James and did not look up. Emma tried again, this time giving several urgent barks and dashing into the water, which at last interrupted our preoccupation with the salmon.

The boat was already out of reach, bobbing on the waves, and in it were all our fishing bags, my rod and the lunch basket. On the bank were one cross husband, one mortified wife and a golden retriever who decided to go to ground in view of the acrimonious exchange which ensued.

There was no doubt about it, it was my fault; I had been in charge of the boat. I thought I had dragged it far enough up the shingle to be secure, but obviously I had not, and now I was going to have to retrieve it from the far end of the lake.

This exercise was not nearly so simple as it sounds. For one thing, we were not on the road side of the lake, so that the terrain was difficult in heavy waders. For another, it was necessary to walk some distance inland and to negotiate various hazards - brambles, barbed wire, streams and areas of bog.

It took me the best part of an hour to be reunited with our wayward craft, which had come to rest against a reed bed so that I had to ask a friendly angler in a nearby boat to give it a shove off with an oar. While all this was going on and I was quietly fuming, the skies darkened. As I got into the boat and prepared to row back the wind got up and before long I found that I was making little headway. Then there was the first flash of lightning and the first - almost simultaneous - clap of thunder.

Once a storm gets into mountains like that it seems unable to extricate itself, going round and round, reverberating terrifyingly. I told myself that the boat and oars were of wood, that my waders were rubber and that I could not be struck. Had I known more about it at the time I might not have been quite so sanguine. I felt sure that James would be feeling extremely guilty and certainly would be worried about me. I bent to the oars, the rain lashing against my back, keeping a more or less straight course to the little bay where James and Emma waited.

Was I welcomed back with open arms? Not exactly, although Emma seemed pleased to see me. If James had been concerned for my safety he certainly didn't show it. He had been left on the bank with only his rod, the net and one very chewed and bedraggled Stoat's Tail, with which he had succeeded in landing a brace of sea trout in my absence. There was virtually no cover on that side of the lake and he and Emma were extremely wet.

"I doubt if you'll ever let a boat get away again," he said, and I must say that he was right, I never have. If anything I go to the other extreme, fussing about pegs and painters until I drive him to distraction. In case you are wondering - yes, I still do all the rowing.

Worms

Confession may be good for the soul, but it plays havoc with the reputation. However...

Late one hot and sunny April Joe Rudd, our invaluable gillie, watched us fish a low and falling Wye, acquiring suntans but nothing else. We only had four days, and on the third James' nerve broke. After another blank morning he said 'Joe, what have I to do to catch a fish?'

'Bait, sir,' replied Joe firmly. 'It's our only chance. Give me your spinning tackle and I'll fix you up.'

I departed upstream leaving them to it. Joe joined me later; he had left James trotting a worm down a nice run. 'Taken to it very well, he has,' said Joe.

'Worms,' I said. 'Yuk.'

During the afternoon James landed two nice fresh salmon, both about 10 pounds. So much for the theories about lady anglers and pheromones.

Next morning - our last - it was hotter and brighter than ever. James used bait without even an offer. During lunch a salmon rolled close in to our bank and Joe, desperate for me to catch a fish, suggested the unthinkable. If I were prepared to do exactly as instructed I might well take a fish, even in such unpromising conditions.

'Anything,' I said, by now willing to sell my soul to the Devil.

Joe put up my spinning rod, using a small metal ball, a couple of swivels, a nylon trace and a proper worm hook. From a moss-filled tin he produced two large worms, threaded them on the hook, and handed me the rod.

'Much more to worming than people think,' he said. 'This is called a link-ledger. Lob the whole lot well out into the current; leave the click off and keep a metre of line loose in your hand. The weight will sink to the bottom and the worms will float downstream. By raising and lowering the rod tip you can make the weight bump along the bottom.'

I did as I was told and soon mastered the art of trotting the worms down the current.

'Now,' said Joe. 'If you feel a twitch, just let the fish take the slack line. Don't do a thing until the line moves away. Then put on the click, raise the rod-point and tighten.

Joe stood at my shoulder making encouraging noises. From time to time he put on fresh worms and I cast them out again. Nothing. He insisted that the pool always held fish; if I were patient, sooner or later something was bound to happen. Much later, the tip of my rod twitched, almost imperceptibly at first and then quite definitely so that it was quivering.

'Joe,' I whispered, hoarse with excitement. 'Something's at my worms.'

He urged me to wait. The line moved sluggishly out of my hand. 'Now,' said Joe. 'Put the click on and raise the rod.'

I did so and, sure enough, I was into a fish. At any moment I expected to feel the familiar rush of a lively springer, but there was nothing of the sort, just a mild pulling. The fish came quickly to the net and it was most certainly not salmo salar, rather leuciscus cephalus - a surprised-looking chub of about 2 pounds. Lightly hooked, it was returned to the river none the worse for its experience.

Joe was bitterly disappointed, but it was time for us to go. What I wanted to know was, to whom did my soul belong? If to the Devil, he still owed me a salmon.

I met the devil on the banks of the Wye again the following year. Not Lucifer himself, of course, but one of his personable young trainee devils. It was again late April, but conditions could not have been more different - bitterly cold, an east wind and sleet showers.

I greeted him civilly, for one can never be too sure about devils, even young, unqualified novices. 'Good morning, Sir,' I said. 'I've come for my fish.'

He smiled. 'What fish?'

I refreshed his memory. 'Last year you said, through your representative - Joe, our gillie - that if I fished diligently with a worm I would be rewarded with a salmon. However, all I

81

caught was a chub. A fine, plump chub it was, to be sure, but nevertheless, no substitute for the King of Fish.'

'Dear me,' he said. 'How very disappointing. You with your fine sensibilities too.'

'Quite a small salmon would do,' I said. 'Ten pounds, or thereabouts. Nothing spectacular. I don't want to break any records.'

He pondered in silence for a while, then spoke again. 'These are not the best possible conditions, and as you know, there have been no salmon caught for more than a week. However, I could arrange for you to catch a fish, if you would be prepared to use a worm again.'

'Done,' I said. I explained that on returning home last year I had confessed to having employed methods despised by many game fishermen and I was aware that as a consequence my reputation had been somewhat sullied. 'And all for nothing,' I said. 'From purist to pragmatist in one quick jump and you failed to deliver the goods.'

The young devil said that in his opinion confessing was a pretty stupid thing to do in any circumstances. Nothing was ever gained from it as far as he could see.

I fished the worm that morning as the wind rose and sleet slanted down, so that I could hardly see out of my polaroids. At intervals I replenished the bait and cast it out into the pool. The current brought it round nicely and I could feel the weight bobbing along the bottom.

At last, the rod-tip quivered as a fish took the worms; the spare line in my left hand went out steadily, I put the click on and struck. The fight was on.

This was no chub. This fish ran and dived and rushed about and I felt the usual palpitations associated with having hooked a salmon. When it eventually came to the net I could see through the mist on my glasses that it was the wrong shape. It flashed bronze instead of silver, and it seemed to have an odd sort of beard.

Joe and James came along the bank at that moment in Joe's van; they rushed over to see my catch.

'Barbel,' said Joe. 'Coarse fishermen put them in years ago. Damned nuisance they are - destroy the salmon redds. They fight well, though, and they go up to 10 pounds. Never mind, have another try. Go down the pool again.'

I said I was much too cold and suggested we go and brew up a nice pot of tea on Joe's stove.

James, also fishing with worms, said 'I'll just have a couple of casts while the kettles boiling'.

He went to the exact spot where I had fished so carefully. His second cast was taken by a 12 pound salmon, which Joe netted for him.

I'm not having any more truck with devils; they are not to be trusted.

I shall stick to the fly, or a spinner, in future.

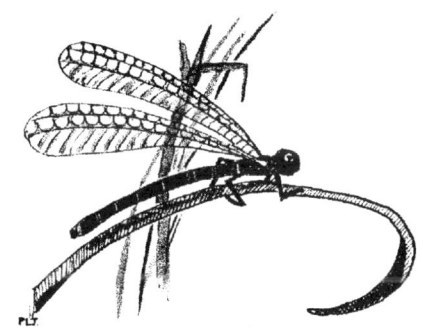

The cold cure

Tom Watt was a salmon fisherman manqúe. As a small boy he had netted sticklebacks from a brook near his home. At the age of seven his father had given him his first trout rod, a well balanced 6.5ft wand that fitted into his hand perfectly. At the same time he was taught to cast a fly, and in that same brook he fished for small brown trout. Later he graduated to a river, getting to know its pools and glides, places where plump trout might lie and be persuaded to take a skillfully presented fly. He became adept at casting under bushes and overhanging branches and soon was a competent trout angler. Listening to his father and his friends, he heard about salmon and he sat wide-eyed as they told of their exploits on huge rivers far away. He was quite determined that one day he would stand on the bank of some mighty river and know what it was like to play the king of fish.

However, at the age of eleven life began in earnest and school, cricket and rugby claimed all his attention, so that opportunities for fishing became more and more limited. During the summer holidays his rod would be taken out and put to good use, and while he stood on the river bank, pleased that his hand had not lost its cunning, he would promise himself that he would do this more often. An insatiable reader, Tom consumed all the fishing stories in his father's books and magazines and he still fervently hoped that one day he would experience the joy of hooking and landing a salmon.

Events conspired against these youthful dreams, for Tom married, produced a family, moved to the city and rose steadily in his profession, so that gradually all thoughts of fishing faded. But it so happened that one day he was drawn into conversation with two friends at his work. They seemed to manage their leisure time rather better than he and they were off to the South of Ireland in the spring to fish for salmon. They went there every year; there were three miles of good fishing owned by a small hotel, run by a Mrs Mary-Ann Rafferty, who made them very welcome and comfortable. They always booked the fishing a year in advance, it was not wildly expensive and why couldn't Tom go with them? It was true that it was a long journey, but it was well worth the trouble and they had never yet come home empty-handed.

At first the whole project seemed impossible; for one thing Tom had no suitable tackle, only possessing a couple of old trout rods and several boxes of trout flies. That, they assured him, was no impediment at all since they had enough equipment between them to supply him with everything he needed for the trip. As time went by the idea grew on him, and when even his wife urged him to go he was finally persuaded.

Eventually the great day dawned. The trio packed the car and set off happily from the South of England, up the M4 motorway to Cardigan, then on to Fishguard, where they put the car on the ferry, established themselves in their cabins and then had dinner before settling down for the night. In the morning they disembarked at Rosslare and set out on the long drive through Wexford and along the winding roads of Waterford to a village that was so small and tucked away that it did not even appear on the map.

Tom had never seen countryside so green and lush. Throughout the long journey his friends regaled him with tales of great struggles with salmo salar, reliving for his pleasure - and their own - past triumphs. Tom, with his vivid imagination, could see it all, and there was no doubt in his mind that this was his chance to fulfil his dearest boyhood ambition.

They stopped for some refreshment at a wayside pub and were well received by the locals when they heard that the three friends were there for the fishing. "Sure," they said. "Wasn't Ireland the best place for fishing in the world, and the salmon so eager to take a fly that they practically climbed up the banks." The bread and cheese, washed down with glasses of dark, velvety Guinness, was the best that Tom had ever tasted.

If there was one small cloud on the horizon it was that by the time they reached Mary-Ann Rafferty's hotel in the late afternoon Tom was not feeling very well. Since leaving the pub earlier he had developed a nasty scratchy sensation in his throat and pricking behind the eyes. He hoped that his discomfort had been produced by the journey and fatigue - after all, they had been travelling for the best part of two days - and that an early night would see him in good order in the morning, but he feared the worst.

Poor Tom was unable to do justice to the gargantuan breakfast of bacon, eggs and fried wheaten farls the next morning. As Mrs Rafferty piled their plates high she observed that it was 'a fine soft morning for the river'. And so it was; there was a nice steady drizzle, just perfect for salmon fishing. But Tom was in trouble. His symptoms had developed overnight until now he had a blinding headache, a sore throat and he felt feverish. He had one of his ghastly colds, he told his friends. It didn't happen often, but when it did they were real humdingers. Also, he had been stupid in not bringing any medicaments with him. Unperturbed by this, they said there was a little village shop nearby and it would be only a matter of minutes to go and buy something to relieve his affliction.

It was the sort of shop that sold everything from groceries and haberdashery to tobacco. Old Mrs Donovan had no aspirins and none of the modern remedies, but she was quite certain she had just the thing, if only she could put her hand on it. "And a grand cure it is," she assured the suffering Tom as she disappeared under the counter.

The three were becoming restive. It was, they pointed out, important that they get to the river as quickly as possible; they did not want to waste good fishing time. Old Mrs Donovan was not to be hurried. "Bless you, sirs," she said. "What's a handful of minutes in the passing of a day?" Just as they were about to give up, she found it - a large bottle on a high, dusty shelf. She climbed down from her ladder, brushed off the cobwebs and gave it to Tom. It bore the legend 'Old Mother Murphy's Cold Cure'. Most of the writing on the label had been obliterated by age, and Tom asked her about the dosage and how often he should take it. "A sup whenever you feel the need," was the reply.

Once on the river the friends parted company. Tom was left to fish the upper bridge pool, which had an easy bank with good wading and plenty of room for a back-cast, while the others made their way upstream to old, familiar haunts. They had checked all Tom's equipment carefully and had made sure he knew exactly what to do if he hooked a salmon. He was to keep the rod-point well up, to get out of the water and to get downstream of the fish. Most importantly, he was to call out and, as they were not far away, they would come to his assistance.

First of all Tom broached his bottle of cold cure, removing the cork, tipping it up, swallowing a large mouthful of the soothing liquid and replacing the bottle carefully in his poacher's pocket. He got into the water quietly, only up to his knees since he was wearing thigh waders, and let out line gradually. He made a few tentative casts, becoming more confident all the time. Really, he thought, this was not all that different from trout fishing, except that everything was on a larger scale. As he fished he took regular sups from his bottle. After a time he felt much better; his cold had made him rather light-headed, he thought, and there was an air of unreality about the morning. He felt as if he were floating, completely at one with his surroundings, part of the river, the grassy banks and the trees. The small grey bridge seemed to be moving gently as the water rippled towards it, slapping at the lichen covered stones on its way to the distant sea. As he made his slow and careful way down the pool he had the strongest feeling that some where a large silver salmon was just waiting for his fly to move over its lie.

Then it happened. A shock went up his right arm, he instinctively tightened, raised the rod-point and the fish was hooked. He saw it jump far out in the river, almost against the opposite bank. Everything seemed to be happening in slow motion and in a mist. He called out, just once, but he was so hoarse that his voice was no more than a croak.

Somehow Tom did all the right things. He waded ashore, got below the salmon and kept a steady pressure on the fish, which moved about slowly in mid-stream. However, after ten minutes or so it suddenly turned and proceeded to run downstream. Tom had not considered the bridge and, too late, he realised that his salmon intended to run through the arch. Only one thing seemed possible in the circumstances. In his euphoric state, Tom shed his jacket and, holding the rod high aloft he took to the river again. He was only faintly aware of the cold water. As in a dream he stumbled towards the bridge, the water well over his waders and up to his waist. Still the fish kept going. Through the bridge it went, followed by Tom.

It was extremely fortunate that his friends had chosen this moment to make sure that Tom was all right, and that they were making their way down the bank towards him as this drama was being played out. They arrived just as he disappeared under the arch. Running up the bank, over the stile and on to the road that ran beside the river, they found a suitable place on the bank past the bridge, downstream of Tom. Rushing down on to the shingle, they waved their arms and shouted "Wade down here and get out of the water."

More by luck than judgement, Tom regained the bank near his friends and sat down heavily, his head spinning, but the rod still held high in his quivering hands. The fish ceased its headlong rush towards the sea, turned and wallowed close to the near bank, where it was netted quickly with very little ceremony by one of his friends. When it was dispatched they turned their attention to Tom, who was an interesting shade of slate grey and shivering uncontrollably. They retrieved his jacket, jog-trotted him to the car and drove quickly to the hotel. Mrs Rafferty fussed over Tom, feeding him hot drinks liberally laced with good Irish whiskey, and got him into bed with three hot water bottles. During the rest of the day, while his friends fished, Tom slumbered peacefully, occasionally waking to take further draughts of his cold cure.

He remembers getting down to the river. He will remember to his dying day the feel of his first salmon taking the fly, the plunge into the icy river, the sight of his friends hurtling down the bank to net his fish, but he has no recollection whatsoever of the next two days.

As Tom lay in a deep sleep, the following morning Mrs Rafferty and his friends were so worried about him that they called in Dr O'Flynn, the dispensary doctor of the village. He examined the almost comatose Tom, and the bottle from which he had derived so much comfort.

"Sure, I'm not surprised you can't wake him," he said. "Old Mother Murphy was taken off the market years ago. It's about 90 per cent laudanum - Tincture of Opium - and he's drunk enough to put a horse to sleep for a week. Just leave the poor decent man alone and let him sleep it off."

Dr O'Flynn tried to remove the bottle, but even in his sleep Tom had it clutched to his chest and would not be parted from it.

When he finally regained full consciousness two days later, Tom felt rested, very hungry and his cold had gone. The bottle was empty. He announced that he was ready to consume a large breakfast and return to the river.

He fished all morning without incident, but, feeling a little weary after lunch and encouraged by his friends to take things easy for a while, he returned to the hotel for an afternoon nap. The next day he hooked, played and landed another salmon, this time the whole performance being in sharp focus and in a more textbook fashion. His friends also had two salmon each and it was agreed that the trip had been most successful, except that they were concerned because Tom had missed two days good fishing. He, however, was well pleased; not only had he salmon to his credit, but they were all three booked in with Mrs Rafferty for the next year.

On the morning of their departure Tom was missing for half an-hour after breakfast. His friends, busy packing the car, wondered where he was, but he soon arrived - beaming, carrying three large bottles of Old Mother Murphy's Cold Cure. It was, he said, Mrs Donovan's entire stock and while his supply lasted he wouldn't fear catching cold. Marvellous stuff. He had never known a cold go so quickly or so pleasantly. He wrapped the bottles carefully and packed them in a suitcase. They made their farewells and set off for home.

That same day it occurred to Dr O'Flynn that perhaps he should visit Mrs Donovan to confiscate what remained of her illegal hoard. He was too late.

"The nice gentleman staying with Mrs Rafferty for the fishing came in this morning. Didn't he climb up the ladder himself and find the only three bottles left to take back across the water? Said there was no medicine the like of it in England."

Dr O'Flynn didn't doubt it. He only hoped Tom wouldn't be arrested by Customs for drug running.

Any luck?

Dangerous as it may be to generalize, I think I am safe in saying that gentlemen do prefer blonds.

Our party had, as usual, booked the fishing for a week in a small West Country hotel which in those days had a nice run of spring salmon. We were three pairs of husbands and wives and, on this occasion, we had been joined by another angling friend and his new wife, whom we had not yet met, one regular pair having dropped out.

Let us call the new wife 'Blondie' to save any embarrassment about names, although that is far too frivolous a sobriquet for such a divine creature. Her hair would have put ripe corn to shame; her eyes were impossibly blue - perhaps lapis lazuli would best describe them - and she curved in all the right places.

I suppose we fishing wives had become a little careless over the years; we were all-purpose, heavy-duty types in comparison, and although we did our best after a day's slithering up and down muddy river banks, we were not too worried if in the evenings we would not have qualified for the cover of Vogue. Blondie was immaculately turned out and appeared on the first night in a little black dress and fragile, strappy sandals that showed off slim ankles to perfection. She looked absolutely stunning, and whatever we other wives may have felt secretly, the men perked up quite miraculously in her presence.

Blondie did not appear at breakfast. She was not fishing, but was quite happy to rise late and then motor round visiting antique shops, of which there are dozens in that part of the world. While we had breakfast as early as possible to get to grips with the river, she slept on.

The first day started well enough. Quite early James hooked and landed a fresh 12 pound salmon in Oak Pool. He came along the bank, beaming with pleasure, for the first fish of the season, played and landed in classic style on a fly of one's own design, is a particular joy. However, before long the smile had turned to a slight frown.

"My waders are leaking," he announced. "They must have perished and walking has made them crack."

There are few more uncomfortable things on a raw March day than wet feet, particularly when it is still quite early in the morning and when one is two fields and a car journey from the hotel. The only prospect is to soldier on with extremities like blocks of ice rather than waste good fishing time. The waders had received proper treatment - hanging in a dark place all winter and stuffed with newspaper - and they had been checked before leaving home, which made him even more cross.

By one-o'clock he was cold, in acute discomfort and looking forward to lunch. When we got to the fishing hut he sighed with relief as he emptied his waders and wrung out his socks. Alas, we had been given the wrong lunch basket. We had ordered ham sandwiches, fruit and mushroom soup, but my first foray into the basket produced cheese sandwiches, liberally spread with chutney. James loathes chutney, or anything hot or spiced.

"Never mind," I said consolingly, trying to scrape the cheese free from the offending goo, "you can have the soup, that'll warm you up."

As I opened the flask I could smell that it was not cream of mushroom. It was not cream of anything, but a ferocious curried concoction which had been specially prepared for another member of the party whose stomach lining was known to be much more resilient than either of ours. There was no milk for tea either.

During the afternoon I got into a salmon - lively and fresh up from the sea. It took a bit of handling, standing as I was on an awkward promontory, but after about half-an-hour it was safely in the net and weighed 15 pounds.

The last straw was that James had three salmon on and off. After each he re-tied with a new fly, checking the hooks carefully, but to no avail. His language was quite dreadful, and it was more than my life was worth to offer any sympathy.

We made our way home, parked the car and made for the rod-room, with me trailing a few yards behind, clomping across the courtyard in my studded waders. I was tired and somewhat dispirited, and probably that mottled blue-red colour which comes from exposure to a bitter wind. At the front door stood a radiant Blondie, swathed in scarlet cashmere, ready to greet her man home from his day in the great outdoors. First of all she accosted James. "Any luck?" she asked sweetly. I flinched, for as well as his other foibles - with which even he will agree he is amply endowed - he has a great antipathy for that question, considering as he does that luck has nothing whatever to do with it. Skill, yes. Luck, no.

He drew himself up to his full six feet and addressed her, coldly. "Madam," he said. "I do not consider that I have been unduly favoured by fortune, but if you mean have I caught any fish yes, I have." And with this he swept past her into the hotel, leaving a trail of wet footprints and small pools of water.

The elegant eyebrows lifted just a fraction and I felt that I must do something to retrieve the situation. Fishing, I explained, does not always bring out the best in some people, particularly those who have had a trying day. My husband was really very nice, with some extremely laudable qualities, but his waders had leaked, he had gone without lunch, he was cold and wet and had lost three salmon. To cap it all, my fish was a good three pounds heavier than his. When he had immersed himself in a hot bath, when he was dry shod and had a glass of something alcoholic in his hand, then he would be restored to his usual benevolent self.

To give Blondie her due, she knew how to charm. When they met again in the bar before dinner she gave James the full benefit of her large blue eyes and said she was sorry to have been so stupid; of course it was a silly question, she realized that now and she would know better in future. She knew she had a lot to learn about fishing and fishermen and she would be most grateful for some help from an expert like him. We other wives managed to keep straight faces only with the greatest difficulty. Blondie then turned her attention to me, saying how wonderful it was to be able to fish, and how she envied me my salmon. She thought perhaps she should try, but first she would need some proper lessons because it wouldn't be fair on others to waste good fishing time trying to teach a complete beginner. By the time we went into dinner all was sweetness and light again.

I have done Blondie a great injustice, of course. I have made her sound like an empty-headed, merely decorative person, which she most certainly is not. She did take up fishing, availing herself of the undivided attention of a proper professional coach, who was heard to say that he felt he should be paying her for the privilege of teaching her to cast - she has that effect on men. She and her husband became regular members of our party.

While it is true that she is never quite as bedraggled as the rest of us, tending on even the worst fishing days to look like the girl who models Barbour jackets, a river bank in rain, wind and snow sometimes does just take the edge off her ultra-polished appearance. More than that, she catches her fair share of fish and has turned out to be very good company. Blondie is a wicked mimic, and whenever the opportunity arises she does a perfect imitation of James, drawing herself up to her full height and with an icy look saying "Sir (or Madam, as the case might be)'. I do not consider that I have been unduly favoured by fortune, but if you mean have I caught any fish, yes I have."

So, if you should come across a beautiful blond angler on the river bank, don't ask her if she has had any luck - you are liable to get a very dusty answer.

Etiquette

There is much more to game fishing than is immediately obvious. Quite apart from choosing the right tackle, learning to cast, knowing the basics about flies, breaking strains of nylon and all the other minutiae of the sport, the angler needs to have a good working understanding of rivers, lakes, weather, insects, animals, birds, and, of course, fish. Finally there is, or should be, a whole world of etiquette.

My crash course in the conventions of angling was a revelation to me, particularly since it came when I was introduced so unexpectedly to fishing on our honeymoon. It seemed that there were two main headings - ALWAYS and NEVER. Always keep off the skyline. Always give other anglers a wide berth. Boat always gives way to bank. Spinner always gives way to fly. (Well, almost always. Obviously you are not expected to get out of the river and defer to someone with a fly rod if you are already half-way down a pool). Never walk near anyone's back-cast. Never speak to an angler unless spoken to. Never, never approach anyone who is playing a fish unless he asks for assistance. Never ask an angler if he has had any luck, since this implies that fortune rather than skill determines his catch.

All this, and much more, I absorbed, to the extent that at first I was terrified of being seen or heard at all. Men can get away with conversation on the river bank, but the ladies must be invisible and silent or be accused of chattering and wasting good fishing time.

It was some time before I realised that fish are unable to hear voices, only vibrations, but James' oft repeated adage which has its origin in a quite different sport - that 'all good bitches run mute' stung me into silence when fishing, and when I did dare to speak it was in a whisper. Ladies are tolerated so long as they can manage their own equipment, untangle their own nylon, rescue their own flies from high branches, unjam their own reels, do not catch appreciably more fish than the men and are suitably modest when they do happen to latch on to something when everyone else is clean.

Having said that, I have never had any trouble with men on the river bank; they have almost always been kind, generous and helpful, as anglers usually are. In fact, I have only ever come across one real dyed-in-the-wool shocker and, to add to his other failings, he was also a rabid misogynist.

We were staying at an hotel in Wales many years ago, one of our favourite haunts at that time. It stood beside a large lake with feeder streams, bays, reed beds, and it was full of wonderful trout, the truly wild salmo trutta fario, golden brown with red spots on their sides. It was a most beautiful place, miles from anywhere, with mountains sweeping down to the very roadside by the lake. When conditions were right it was possible to come home with good baskets, but the trout were quite choosy and certainly did not take just anything that was presented to them. The proprietor was more than delighted when the guests did well, and as the lake was overcrowded there was no limit to the number one could take.

When we arrived the atmosphere was somewhat gloomier than usual. The proprietor, who was an old friend, had booked in a complete stranger and he said that he along with the other guests had not taken him to their hearts. He was afraid that we might find him a bit hard to bear. Some of the other anglers, most of whom were extremely well known to us, said that the stranger thought nothing of cutting in on other drifting boats, rowing too close to the bank where people were fishing, and of shouting. He was pompous and a braggart and they were thoroughly fed up with him. Altogether he seemed to have made quite an impression in the short time that he had been there, and to everyone's dismay he was booked in for another ten days. He seemed quite impervious to the chill which surrounded him everywhere; quite probably he was used to it.

Also staying there at that time was another old friend of ours, a Rural Dean. He was a white-haired, genial man with a face like a Ruben's cherub, but possessed of a dry sense of humour. He greeted us eagerly.

"Thank goodness you've arrived. You must come and share my table I'm alone, and I've been afraid that awful chap would come and foist himself on me. There are times when I find it difficult to love my fellow man. "

It appeared that the Dean had been reduced to taking his drink into the residents lounge to escape the menace, who monopolised the bar, holding forth to his captive audience. It was essential to him that he should catch the biggest and the most fish, and he talked loudly, whether anyone was listening or not, about his exploits and successes elsewhere, the Welsh hotel comparing very unfavourably, in his view, with other places he had visited.

For the next two days we all endured the menace, keeping as far out of his way as possible. He was heard to remark to the unhappy proprietor that if there was one thing he could not stand it was women fishing. I was the only fishing wife present at the time and I resolved to do my invisible act, but I was aware that James and the Dean were hatching some plot.

Our third morning was what the Irish call 'soft', with a nice steady drizzle, the world grey and green. We rowed down to the bottom of the lake and hauled our boat ashore. James suggested that I should fish from the bank into the edge of the reed bed, always a productive place. He and the Dean, who had also rowed down, positioned themselves one on each side of me, some fifty paces away. The menace was fishing in his boat off a small bay several hundred yards away, just visible in the curtain of mist.

I finally settled on a tiny Peter Ross, having tried various other patterns first, and I killed several trout on that before lunch, also returning, some under the 10 inch limit. From time to time, James or the Dean would walk casually to where I was fishing and surreptitiously put a fish into my bass.

By noon the rain had cleared and the sun came out. We lunched on the bank - flasks of soup, sandwiches, fruit and sherry from the Dean's bottle. "For my stomachs sake," he said with a smile as he poured

However, it wasn't long before the menace arrived to disturb the peace, rowing round the reed bed and hailing us loudly. James pointed out, very acidly, that he was right over our fishing ground, but he took no notice, only shouting to enquire about our morning's catch. The Dean replied that Mrs Armstrong had a few, at which the menace turned away and rowed off. I suggested that perhaps we should spend the afternoon afloat, but James was quite insistent that we should continue from the bank. Again he and the Dean were on each side of me, well spaced out. Our basses were placed together under a tree and every so often they would saunter up to my bass and add to its burden.

Several times the menace rowed up the lake to prepare for another drift away from the reed bed. Twice I had to get my line out of the water quickly because he came so close to the bank, and twice I happened to have a fish on as he passed. I said nothing, but James was moved to inform him in no uncertain terms that he was too near.

I had several nice fish on an Invicta and James added regularly to my catch. The Dean excelled himself by landing a three pound brown trout in perfect condition when he employed a sinking line and a large Coachman, which he proclaimed cheerfully to be a bit sneaky, and that too was added to my collection. Fortunately the basses were the larger size we usually used for salmon and sea trout so that all the fish fitted into one, except the three pounder, which had a piece of string tied through its gills and was carried separately.

James explained that our time of arrival back was critical; we had to aim to get there after the menace had gone ashore and while he was reciting his day's feats to the other guests, who were sitting outside the hotel with their drinks in the evening sunshine. Our timing was perfect; as we disembarked at the jetty the menace was in full flow. At some pre-arranged signal, not previously known to me, the Dean and the proprietor engaged in a little play-acting. The Dean announced that Mrs Armstrong had a very nice basket and one particularly good fish. As I tottered towards the group with my heavy, bulging bass and the Dean's three pounder the proprietor produced his camera, insisting that I should spread my catch out on the grass and stand behind them with my rod.

"Smile please," he said as the shutter clicked on the fish, all twenty-one of them.

James and the Dean strolled, nonchalantly and unnoticed, with their empty basses to the refrigeration room, and when they were asked later how they had done said that they had had a few but that they had been outclassed. The menace became caught up in the throng, the proprietor insisting that he come and see what the lake could produce when fished by an expert. Some of the other anglers joked about the inadvisability of letting ladies fish and taunted the menace about having his eye so thoroughly wiped. It was all too much for him. He was absolutely furious, although he himself had six or seven good trout. He pushed his way through the crowd and stalked into the hotel.

The menace came down to dinner later than usual, by-passing the bar and, for once, quiet. He asked the proprietor to prepare his bill because he intended to leave first thing in the morning. After dinner he went straight to his room. When we came down to breakfast the next day he had already gone. Clearly everyone was delighted and the whole atmosphere was one of relief, but I said I felt rather guilty at my role in his premature departure.

"Nonsense, my dear," said the Dean. "Only doing God's work. Hebrews Ch 12 v 6."

I went and looked it up in my bedside Gideon. 'For whom the Lord loveth he chasteneth'.

Merry as the marriage bell

I doubt very much if the place exists any longer. For one thing, paying guests have become more concerned with their creature comforts these days; for another, there is less tolerance of eccentrics now.

The fishing pub was owned by an elderly major, who ran on very high octane. I personally never saw him sober, and I am not convinced that this would have been an advantage, but he was generally accepted as a 'character' who was fine if he liked you, but was quite capable of throwing guests out at any hint of criticism. The pub itself was seventeenth century and in sore need of attention. Its ancient thatch was home to rodents, roosting and nesting birds and unspeakable creepy crawlies; threadbare carpets rose from warped floorboards with an icy draught whenever the front door was opened and every board and beam creaked alarmingly, particularly in the long watches of the night. The major's wife, who was by no means teetotal herself, and a couple of local girls did their best to keep the place in some sort of order. The fact that the Major owned several miles of very good salmon fishing was his saving grace.

Staying there that midsummer were just five people - James, myself, a friend of ours and a young honeymoon couple, Charles and Kate. The young man confided to us that he had first fished only two years before and subsequently had taken the precaution of teaching his fiancée to fish before actually marrying her. She seemed to like it, he said, although her success so far had been confined to small trout from a brook. He himself now devoted all his spare time to fishing. He had been fortunate enough to be taken to Ireland the year before, where, on the Blackwater, he had killed his first salmon. He was hoping to repeat the performance on this holiday. We observed that the conditions were good, a little bright and warm, perhaps, for complete perfection, but we wished him well.

One evening after dinner there was some discussion about landing salmon. I sat listening to the comparative merits and demerits of netting, tailing, beaching, gaffing and hand-tailing. The newly-weds sat by the inglenook, fingers intertwined, and I thought what a pretty girl Kate was. Our friend asked what was to be done in case of dire emergency. Suppose, he said, just for example, a lady who was not strong enough to hand-tail a sizeable fish, found herself without the aid of a net, tailer or gaff, with no convenient shingle beach nearby, with a salmon hooked and well out in the stream and a husband clutching the rod and demanding that she do something. Obviously, said James, she should take the rod and play the fish while the man went into the river and hand-tailed it.

"Suppose she refused to take the rod in case she lost the fish?" persisted our friend. "What then?" I suspected that our friend was speaking from some previous traumatic experience, and the whole thing was beginning to sound like the man with a very small boat, a fox, a goose and a bag of corn to be ferried across a river. James, as usual, had the answer. There was, he said, only one thing to be done. The lady should remove her trousers, tie knots in the legs about the knees and, using the garment as a net, capture the fish in its top. Simple. He claimed to have seen this done and declared that on rare occasions it might be the only way.

The conversation continued, consisting mainly of amusing anecdotes of bizarre and unlikely goings-on on river banks. I sat deep in a comfortable armchair, replete after a pleasantly tiring day in the fresh air and some excellent roast beef, half drowsing. I had, after all, heard it all before. The newly-weds listened, covertly holding hands.

The following afternoon I visited a famous local garden instead of fishing. When I arrived back at the pub in time for dinner everyone seemed to be subdued and furtive. Yes, they had caught salmon; James and our friend had one each, and Charles had hooked a real beauty in Foxes Pool and ultimately it had been landed safely. From the lowered voices and oblique glances I gathered that something untoward had happened. Where was the Major and why was he not at his usual welcoming station behind the bar?

The Major, apparently, had collapsed from - as the Irish would say - 'having drink taken'. Kate had retired to bed with a headache. Charles had gone out, muttering something about night fishing for sea trout he had appeared with an enormous bruise on his forehead, which he said was caused by a hairbrush which had slipped out of his wife's hand. The Major's wife, in a highly emotional state, was busy having hysterics in the kitchen. She was only pacified when we assured her that soup and sandwiches would do admirably for dinner and that we would help ourselves in the bar, keeping a strict account for the Major.

Later, James and our friend related the events of the afternoon. Charles had hooked a salmon in Foxes Pool, and, after a few jumps, it ran downstream. Being new to the water, and inexperienced, he did not realise until it was too late that some forty yards below him the river turned in a sharp dogleg to the left, the water deepening abruptly, and that there was a substantial buttress of earth bank between him and the next pool. He was standing well out in the river when he first made contact, and, thinking to play it in the classical manner, waded towards the shore to get out of the water. The fish suddenly took off and ran downstream, turning the corner into the next pool. As a result, his line encountered the jutting bank and actually embedded itself in the soft earth. Quickly he made his way out into the river again, but the line remained buried in the earth bank. This gave rise to acute anxiety since, although the line moved freely in the runnel it had made, Charles could not get it out of its earthy groove because of the acute corner. Thus, he was in one pool and the fish was out of sight in another downstream, and there appeared no way that the twain were likely to meet. He was quite sure that sooner or later the line would break. He called urgently to his wife to go down to the next pool with the net, to wade in - taking no heed of the fact that she would get thoroughly wet - and to net his fish, which was wallowing about, more or less exhausted.

To give the poor girl her due, she tried. The fish was out in the middle of the stream, well out of sight of her husband.

Unfortunately, as she waded out she dropped the net. We all know what happens when something is dropped into a river - it disappears, usually forever. She screamed that she had lost the net and now had nothing with which to get the fish.

Charles' attention had not been entirely on his beloved in the lounge the evening before, for he remembered what had been said about capturing a salmon in difficult circumstances. He called Kate back to him in the upstream pool so that he could give her precise instructions in as calm a manner as he could muster. She was to remove her trousers, knot the legs at the knees, then wade out and trap the salmon in the top of her trousers, as in a net.

Kate scampered back round the curve of the bank, did as instructed and plunged back into the river, where the salmon, all but played out, still swirled about sluggishly on the surface.

Five minutes later, James and our friend arrived to find the girl dredging her trousers at the exhausted salmon, which stubbornly refused to be trapped in this makeshift net. Taking in the situation at once, they dashed out into the river in their chest waders, tailed the salmon and brought it ashore triumphantly. There was a noisy exchange with the still invisible Charles to the effect that now they had cut the nylon he could reel in and come to admire his catch. Congratulations were exchanged with a very relieved and delighted young man.

In the heat of the moment they failed to notice that Kate had disappeared. Charles, the bit now thoroughly between his teeth, declared his intention to continue fishing. James and our friend, because they had to pack ready to leave first thing in the morning, decided to make their way back to the pub.

There was no such thing as 'hours' in that establishment, and by the time the pair arrived back Kate and the Major were well settled in the bar. Kate clad in what appeared to be one of the Major's dressing gowns, was alternately raging, hicupping and sobbing. The Major, who was plying her with alcohol, was at his most maudlin and was weeping with her.

The bar was so placed that it was impossible to get from the front door to the stairs without passing through it. James and our friend, completely unaware of what awaited them, walked straight into the hornet's nest. On seeing them, Kate launched into a tirade.

"There I was," she cried, "Standing for all practical purposes starkers in the middle of the river, struggling with those bloody trousers. And you two great oafs don't even look at me, let alone offer to help me. No, you brushed me aside to get at that damned fish. And Charles was just as bad - he only looked at the salmon. He didn't even ask me if I was all right. Nobody offered me a jacket- I might not have been there for all the notice anyone took of me. So I wrapped myself in the car rug and drove back here".

"I can tell you this," she went on furiously. "If that's the way fishermen behave in the presence of nude ladies, if that's what fishing does to men I want no part of it. More than that, I certainly don't want to be married to anyone who fishes."

At this point the Major's wife joined the party. James and our friend slunk quietly upstairs, leaving all three weeping into their pink gins.

We left after breakfast the next morning, by which time the Major had been roused from his stupor and, like his wife, was suffering from a monumental hangover. There was no sign of either Charles or Kate.

Did the marriage survive? I have no idea, but I have often wondered.

The angler's curse

We knew the lake well; its reed beds, bays and small feeder streams, its deeps and shallows. It lay in a long, narrow valley with Cader Idris casting a shadow over its waters on one side: on the other, gentler hills sloped down to the road which wound along its banks.

We had seen the lake in all its moods, sometimes drifting gently with light breezes and sometimes being buffeted by high winds and driving rain, when white horses rode its surface and it took us both, each at an oar, pulling furiously, to get the boat back safely to the hotel jetty.

We had set out before dawn, crossing England, and,after driving through small Welsh villages and over a mountain pass, at last the lake lay below us, glittering in the early morning sunshine. It seemed the most beautiful sight in the world and the hotel on its banks promised a welcome and a much-needed breakfast.

At breakfast we met various other fishermen, some of whom were old friends, and they were less than ecstatic. The senior angler shook his head sadly.

"The lake's not fishing too well at the moment. Can't think what's wrong. I've had two small trout in three days and no-one else has done any better."

James was sure that this was due to man's ineptitude rather than any fault with the lake, and he was quite certain that things would change for the better now that we had arrived. Wild brown trout had always been prolific there, not always easy to catch, to be sure, but morning and evening rises never failed and it was a poor day that did not yield good baskets.

We were so eager to be on the lake that we did not even stop to unpack. We need not have been in such a hurry, although it was very pleasant drifting in the boat. We renewed our long-standing acquaintance with the two resident swans, simply called Pen and Cob, so graceful on the water, so ungainly as they waddled up at lunchtime to be fed. James would lecture them gently on their diet as they took bread from his hand, informing them that they should be eating the lake weed and not filling themselves with fisherman's sandwiches. Every year they nested, guarding first eggs and then cygnets with their lives, before driving them off at maturity to find water of their own.

A shepherd was working his dog on a hillside; we could hear his whistle and could see the black and white border collie streaking across a field to collect stray sheep. It was all very peaceful. Emma was lying quietly asleep in the bottom of the boat, but she was always ready to spring up as soon as either of us hooked a fish to supervise proceedings. She knew all about fishing.

We tried various flies - dry, wet, bright, dull, large and small - to no avail. There was a brief, splashy rise on one side of the lake towards evening and James got one fish on a black gnat, but we had no other offers.

There was some lively discussion after dinner that evening, a wide variety of opinions being advanced as to why catches had become so meagre. Poaching and pollution are always the first to be mentioned, swiftly followed by over-fishing, lack of food or disease. As time wore on, suggestions and proposed cures grew increasingly preposterous. The long-suffering proprietor, whose family had owned the hotel, the lake and a hillside farm for many generations, joined us in the bar and listened sympathetically to his disgruntled guests. He knew that the lake had fished perfectly well the week before and would fish perfectly well again soon, but he was far too sensible and good mannered to say so. He received all advice with due solemnity. Yes, perhaps it would be a good thing to get samples taken of the water, the lake bed and the weed to make sure that nothing was wrong. Yes, he would certainly consider re-stocking the lake. Yes, he would have a word with the bailiff about the possibility of poaching.

One of the company, never known to travel without his fly tying equipment, set up his vice in a quiet corner of the bar after dinner and proceeded to produce a sure killer. When completed, this confection had a silver body and a streamer of black and yellow maribou.

"That," he said, "should produce some reaction if there are any fish in the lake."

Another regular visitor was of the opinion that the lake was in dire distress.

"We've got to face it," he said, "the fish are just not there."

At this point James and I, who had had a long and tiring day, went to bed, leaving the arguments going round in circles.

By lunch-time the next day one fish had been caught - on the 'killer'. On inspection it was certainly a large brown trout, but a ghastly looking thing with a long, thin body and a gross, rebarbative head.

"Cannibal," said James in disgust. "Still, I suppose it proves that he was getting well down."

In the afternoon the 'light and variable winds' died completely and the lake was like a mill pond. We sat becalmed. I remembered reading somewhere that an Iron Blue sometimes succeeds in such circumstances, when trout will look at nothing else. I tied one on, but nothing showed any interest.

Suddenly the lake came alive: the water boiled and heaved. Fish came to the surface - not rising at individual flies but cruising along, their backs out of the water and their mouths wide open. They were obviously dredging something from the surface and were oblivious to anything else.

We were soon covered in minute black flies, much too tiny to imitate, and we watched, awestruck, as thousands of fish, all over the lake, were engaged in the same mad orgy of feeding. So intent were they in gorging themselves that they bumped into each other and even into the boat. Other boats dotted about the lake were motionless, while their occupants gazed in wonder about them, only too well aware that they could do nothing but watch.

"What is it? What are they taking?" I asked when I was capable of speech.

James laughed. "Just look at them. No fish in the lake indeed. That's shot that theory down in flames."

"Yes, but what are they taking?"

"They're smutting. Those little black flies are reed smuts" 'The Angler's Curse', but this is the biggest hatch I've seen for years."

I suppose the spectacular display went on for about fifteen minutes, although we lost count of time as we watched, mesmerised. Emma stood, paws on the thwart, gazing overboard in disbelief at the fish and probably wondering why we were not doing something constructive about the situation. Certainly we could have netted some with no difficulty at all.

The proprietor was standing on the jetty with his cine camera, recording the activity on the lake. When the display stopped, almost as quickly as it had begun, he greeted the returning boats, filming the anglers and their reactions. Listening to their comments, I thought what a pity it was there was no sound track to go with the film. When we had all adjourned to the bar, he told us that there were usually small hatches of reed smut on still evenings once or twice a season, but that it was many years since he had seen anything on that scale.

When I asked why the fish had been 'off' for some days before it happened, and why it had all happened so suddenly, I got no very satisfactory answers.

"Perhaps," said one, "they had been feeding sub-surface on the larvae before the exuberant hatch. Who could tell?"

Later I asked James what he thought.

"I think it's a good thing we brought our golf clubs," he said. "We'll go to Aberdovey tomorrow for a couple of rounds. Every fish in the lake is satiated at the moment. Perhaps when they get over their acute indigestion they'll start taking our flies again, like proper Christian trout."

Not enough action

It came as a complete surprise to us when Samuel Stride, Sam to his friends, S.S. to his employees - announced that he proposed to come salmon fishing with us in the spring. For one thing, he was not the outdoor type and had never shown the slightest interest in anything but high finance; for another, the only exercise he ever seemed to get was boarding 'planes for Hong Kong, New York or Geneva.

However, it seemed that Sam had been to have one of those fancy medical check-ups so beloved of executive types and had been told that his way of life was putting too much strain on his blood pressure. He should ease up, perhaps take up fishing.

This had caught Sam's imagination and he was quite determined to do the thing properly and to pit his strength against the best fighter British rivers could offer. I suppose we were at fault to some extent because, like all anglers, we had rather glorified the sport, telling stories of epic struggles with salmon in fast flowing rivers and deep pools - all of which were true, of course, - but we had glossed over the steep banks, brambles, cold, wet, bone-aching fatigue and the days - sometimes weeks - when absolutely nothing happens.

Somewhat to my dismay James agreed that he should come, but insisted that first he must go and have proper casting lessons, which he did, reluctantly and showing little real aptitude.

In the autumn, when we took him trout fishing as a prelude to the spring salmon, James shook his head sadly and said he feared that our friend was, to put it at its best, incurably ham-handed. He just did not seem to be able to control the rod, so that invariably the line, cast and fly landed on the water with a great splash, scaring every fish for miles. He did not take kindly to instruction or to the advice that he should practice on grass.

When it came to choosing tackle for the spring we tried to curb his worst excesses, taking endless trouble to make a list of things he would need, but in spite of this he bought mountains of unnecessary equipment. Money was no object and he considered that what was the biggest and most expensive must be the best.

Next April when we arrived in the West Country the river was in spate, so that James took the opportunity to demonstrate to Sam the mysteries of the fixed-spool spinning reel. He seemed to manage this somewhat better, the technique being much more suited to his personality than the more graceful movements of fly casting.

However, another problem arose because, apart from high - powered telephone calls and board room decisions, Sam was ill equipped to cope with the more mundane aspects of life, such as the workings of any sort of apparatus. He always had minions to ease his path with regard to such trivia. His restless energy did not translate well to the river bank and he was impatient with the actual mechanism of the reel. James explained carefully the action of the fixed-spool reel, how to adjust the clutch, and so on. He explained about the difficulties with nylon; how it could kink, how to prevent this and what to do if it happened. But he was aware, even as he talked, that he had less than half of Sam's attention all this technical stuff being boring and not really essential to the business in hand.

For two days we kept a close eye on Sam. I obliged by tying his spinners on for him and James checked his reel from time to time. Sam lost an amazing number of baits on the opposite bank, up trees and on snags, but this did not worry him in the least since he had bought his spinning baits by the gross. He felt that he was gradually getting the hang of things, but we were less convinced of any progress.

On the afternoon of the third day Sam wandered off by himself, saying that he was exhausted by all the fresh air and unaccustomed exercise and that he would see us back at the hotel. We were vastly relieved because we had spent most of our time rescuing him, his nylon and dozens of spinners from quite unusual situations. We were anxious to do a little undisturbed fishing ourselves.

When we arrived back at the hotel some hours later, there was a nice fresh little salmon already on the slab with a neat label 'S. Stride'. "Good old Sam," we said, delighted. "Let's go and hear all about it."

If we expected him to be in a state of excitement we were disappointed. So, it transpired, was he. Having left us he had walked along the river and, as he passed Willow Pool, he had seen a splash over towards the far bank. He thought he might as well have a few casts there to see if he could get the salmon to take, although he was alone and there was no other angler within earshot.

At least he had the wit to remove his net before wading into the river and to put it down safely on the shingle bank. This was easier said than done because he had insisted on buying a huge net, which was carried between the shoulder blades on a patent quick-release strap, which nobody, least of all Sam, had managed to persuade to work.

There was, he said, a large stone, or something, sub-surface, just where he had seen the fish and he kept getting caught on it. He lost several baits and had to re-tie three or four times.

When his bait stopped again he decided that that was it - he was going to call it a day. He pulled the line to free the spinner and felt a slight movement. It seemed to him that the snag was loose perhaps a branch under the water - and that if he walked backwards slowly he might be able to retrieve his minnow and not lose yards of nylon into the bargain. As he backed slowly towards his net the 'branch' gradually came across the river, into the shallows and almost up on the shingle beach, which was only a few inches under water. The 'branch' was a perfectly good salmon weighing 7 pounds, which, not realising it was hooked, had followed the slight tension like a dog on a lead. By some miracle the hook did not come away, nor did the nylon break, as he continued walking backwards.

Sam beached the fish, snatched up his net and, using the technique employed by small boys catching butterflies, netted it and dragged it on to dry land. Here he dispatched it with his brand new, silver-plated priest, which he carried slung on his belt much in the manner of old-time western gunfighters.

We did not enquire as to how he came to have two large pieces of Elastoplast on the knuckles of his left hand. The total playing time of the fish, he said with disgust, had been less than five minutes.

When we brought our salmon back to the hotel on subsequent days his disbelief at our stories of hard fighting springers was palpable - mere fishermen's tales. His disenchantment with events continued; Sam caught nothing more and his gross of baits shrank rapidly. It was clear that he was pining for the office and for the bustle and commotion of the City. It was also obvious that Sam thought salmon fishing greatly over-rated.

He was again alone when he hooked his second salmon. He had been sitting on the bank reading a book on Corporate Finance, when he thought perhaps he should stretch his legs and get into the river. Most unfortunately, he had not changed the nylon end-to-end as instructed, nor had he bothered to tie on a swivel, nor had he remembered to tie on opposite-spin minnows. In short, he had employed no anti-kink devices for several days. He had not corrected the tension on the reel either, so that there was no resistance when a salmon suddenly pulled off ten yards of line.

So surprised was he at this turn of events that he failed to increase the tension on the clutch, but merely repeated his former ploy of backing away from the fish. As the twisted line passed through the top ring it promptly kinked and wrapped itself into a terrific tangle. Sam backed farther and farther away, trying to exert some pressure on the salmon, but he only succeeded in producing a bigger and bigger birdsnest. He could not reel in because the tangle of line would not go through the top ring. It did not occur to him, not being mechanically minded, to tighten the clutch, or even to hold the line by hand; he just went on re-treating.

After walking parallel to the river for some 40 yards, the shingle ended and he had to stop. He then began to pull line off the reel by hand. Of course, as it came off the reel it kinked even more and quite soon he had 10 yards of nylon wound round the reel, the rod and his arm. finally the whole thing stuck solid and he could not get it free.

At this point he shouted for help and, as luck would have it, two passing anglers heard his cries and came to his assistance. Meanwhile, the salmon had been swimming round in the pool, not greatly alarmed. The senior angler, experienced not only in the ways of salmo salar but also in those of other, less competent fishermen, took in the situation at once. At one end of the shingle was Sam, his rod and reel wrapped inextricably in nylon; from the rod-tip a colossal birdsnest stretched some 40 yards downstream to a fish in the middle of the river.

The angler waded carefully into the water and grasped the line only to find that the salmon too had become trapped in several coils of the heavily kinked nylon, which hampered its attempts to escape. He did the only thing possible in the circumstances; he backed gently out of the river, holding the line, and coaxed the salmon into the shallows. His friend, who had been waiting, poised and ready, promptly tailed it and dragged it ashore. they killed the fish and cut the line at the bait.

Once released, they said, the line seemed to take on a life of its own. It retracted rapidly towards the rod, coiling the while, and then added itself to the tangle already enmeshing Sam, his rod and reel. Apparently it took one of them ten minutes to cut Sam free, while the other insisted on taking photographs of the scene. Sam was definitely not amused. His sole further contribution to the proceedings made with an ill grace and only when they insisted - was to help the other two cut the tangled mass of nylon into inch lengths, thus rendering it harmless to other riverside life.

Sam then bore his fish back to the hotel. We never could agree on the playing time of that particular salmon.

That evening Sam said he didn't much go for fishing; it was all too technical and there was not enough action. He had decided to return to London to get to grips again with the yen, the dollar and the Deutschmark. He left first thing the next morning. To this day he is quite convinced that salmon do not fight, that our tales of titanic struggles with the king of fish are figments of the imagination and that, so far as excitement goes, the Stock Market is infinitely superior to anything a river has to offer.

Life begins at Sixty-five

Retirement can be a time of great enjoyment and personal fulfilment; it can also be a canker in the home. The trouble was that John, like so many others, was quite unprepared for it. There was the usual farewell dinner in his honour, at which he received his gold watch and the thanks of the company for many years devoted and tireless service, but then he faced an unplanned future of idleness.

I have always thought a watch or a clock, however valuable or ornate, to be a particularly insensitive valedictory gift, marking as it does the passing of one of the most desirable fugitive intangibles known to man.

However, time hung heavily on John's hands; he found himself at a loose end with absolutely nothing to do. He had never had any interest at all in ball games, not even in a spectator capacity; gardening bored him to tears; he was averse to any known form of physical exercise; he had no desire to collect objects of any kind, or to travel, and he was no great reader. He became morose and withdrawn.

Peggy, his wife, with whom I played golf occasionally, was not best pleased either. Suddenly she had her husband about the place all day, complaining of paralytic boredom, requesting regular meals and endless cups of coffee It disrupted her routine to such an extent that she was in despair. Clearly, something had to be done, and quickly, so, as an act of mercy, James was persuaded to take John fishing.

As luck would have it, they chose a perfect day; the sun shone - but not too brightly; a gentle breeze ruffled the surface of the lake, birds sang their spring songs and, most important of all, the fish were in an obliging mood.

It had been the intention on that first day just to take him in the boat, to let him row, to get the feel of the thing and to see if he was interested. However, after James had hooked a couple of nice rainbows, which he allowed him to net, John became desperate to try for himself.

Fishing from a boat is not for beginners, so they found a suitable bank with the wind behind and no unfriendly, grasping trees to hinder a backcast. After a short lecture on essentials, such as always wearing glasses, preferably polaroids, when casting, how to put the rod together, how to fit the reel, and so on, a piece of bright red wool was tied to the nylon leader and John was taught to cast. He quickly discovered that it was by no means as simple as it looked: sometimes the nylon lay in an untidy heap in the water and sometimes the line hit the surface so hard that any self-respecting trout would have made for a more peaceful spot. It was rare that everything went out in a nice straight line, but gradually he got the action and the timing better, watching James' demonstration eagerly.

Eventually, James replaced the wool with a proper fly, showing John how to tie it on securely and explaining why he had chosen that particular pattern. John was enthralled. So intent were they both on getting the casting right that I don't think either was anticipating a fish actually taking the Invicta, but, as John was drawing the fly from the water, it was taken and he had a fish on. He tried to keep calm as James talked him through it.

"Keep the rod point up. Let him have line if he wants to run. Keep the rod point up. Take in line when you can. Don't let the line loose. KEEP THE R0D POINT UP."

When the fish came to the net it was a plump rainbow of two pounds.

John was shown how to use the priest, quickly knocking the fish on the head - avoiding the nylon cast. He was then instructed how to remove the fly without getting it tangled in the net.

If that rainbow had been a ten pound salmon John could not have been more pleased. He insisted that it sould be kept separate from James' catch so that there should be no doubt which was his; he was going to share it with Peggy for supper that night. He remained in a happy daze as they returned to the boat, where James quickly caught another trout, completing their allowance of two brace for the day. In the car on the way home John could talk of nothing else but fishing. He was thoroughly hooked.

John set about his new hobby with an almost evangelical fervour. He had proper professional casting lessons; he went to weekend classes all over the country to learn about trout fishing and to meet other anglers. He borrowed and read avidly every book we had on the subject; he bought fishing videos and magazines and sent away for all the catalogues advertised therein. He and James went into endless conclaves about tackle, breaking strains of nylon, knots, the mysteries of cleaning reels and putting them together again afterwards. It became an obsession, but, as he pointed out very reasonably, he had a lifetime of the sport to make up. What a fool he was not to have started earlier, he mourned. If only he had known before.

We introduced John to our fishing club and he also joined another near to his home, so that he was fully occupied all that first season. Peggy was under the impression that they would travel abroad to find some sun for their summer holidays as usual. The Canaries, perhaps. Tenerife. Instead, she found herself at an English lakeside hotel where there was absolutely nothing to do but fish or go for long walks. She was invited to row the boat, but declined this dubious honour as she felt, probably wisely, that it might turn out to be the thin end of a very dangerous wedge. She said, when we enquired about their holiday, that it had been 'restful' and that she had seen John at breakfast and dinner each day. However, she admitted to being vastly relieved at being able to resume something like a normal home life again, although she did wonder what she was going to do with her husband in the winter. We assured her that it was not a problem: even when addicted anglers could not actually put a fly on water they thought about it, dreamt about it and prepared for the forthcoming season. They cleaned their tackle, sorted fly-boxes, re-varnished rods, read books, watched films on the subject and, most time-consuming of all, they tied flies. More than that, John's new hobby - if one could refer to the noble art of angling in such inadequate terms - would solve the family's gift problems for ever. No more boring shirts, ties and socks; instead, well in advance of any anniversary, they would be given heavy hints of items of equipment required.

A conspiracy was hatched to introduce John to fly-tying, and James provided Peggy with a list of all the things he would need. For Christmas she presented him with a fine vice and Jackie Wakeford's beautifully illustrated book. We gave him John Goddard's 'Waterside Guide' and 'The Super Flies of Still Water'.His children and grandchildren weighed in with wools, tinsels, various capes of feathers, dyed squirrel tails, reels of bright silks, hooks, bottles of coloured varnish and all the other materials necessary to the fly-tyer.

There was no stopping him. He attended classes and applied himself wholeheartedly to his task for the next three months, until he had several brand new fly-boxes full of every known type of trout fly, all of which he had tied himself.

Having spent the winter in this manner, John could hardly contain his impatience. During February and March, no matter what the weather, he could be seen on his lawn, rod assembled, practising casting, and on the first day of April he was on the lake at dawn. When he caught his first trout of the new season on a fly of his own tying his happiness was complete.

During that summer John spent every possible moment he could fishing. He took to travelling far and wide to try new water - rivers, lakes or reservoirs - so that a considerable amount of time was spent away from home. Peggy did remark to me, rather wistfully I thought, that she saw less of John now during the trout season than she had when he worked, and summer holidays abroad seemed to be a thing of the past. When I told James, he said there was no pleasing some people. "And anyhow, she hasn't seen anything yet. John is already starting to ask about salmon fishing." He thought for a moment and then went on, "Do you know, there are only about three weeks in the year when it isn't possible to fish for salmon somewhere in the British Isles?"

The Colonel's Thousandth

We saw the Colonel for the last time on a fishing holiday some years ago.

Each autumn we joined a few friends for the last week of the season, meeting at a small fishing hotel on a river which had a late run of salmon and held sea trout. The Colonel was always there.

He was a most remarkable man. Born just before the turn of the century, he was then in his 85th year. He had seen action in both world wars, having employed what he called a 'ruse de guerre' in the first, when he lied about his age to become a pilot in the Royal Flying Corps. He had led a busy and adventurous life, but salmon fishing was his great passion.

That holiday the Colonel was on his 999th salmon - every one caught on a fly and all meticulously documented in his game books. He caught his first at the age of seven with a greenheart rod and an old gut-eyed fly of his father's, with the ghillie holding him by the seat of his pants while he played it. He had encountered salmon in many British rivers. There had been monsters from Tweed, Tay and Spey, hard fighting springers and gentler autumn fish.

Each entry was made on the day of the catch, when it was fresh in the memory. Every detail was set down precisely: date, river, beat, pool, weather conditions, fly, time caught, and comments. The observations were shrewd and illuminating, and often prophetic, and through them it was possible to trace the history of salmon fishing over the past eight decades.

Greenheart rods had given way to split cane. It was recorded that on his fiftieth birthday he had been given the last word in Hardy rods - a double handed J.J.H. Palakona split cane which cost £25, was 14.5 ft long and weighed 27 ounces. Its latest successor was a 14 ft Boron graphite wand weighing a mere 10.5 ounces.

His comments made it clear that he considered the advent of the floating line for summer fishing an unmixed blessing, and he had welcomed the coming of a line which floated without greasing. The development of all sorts of sinking lines was also greeted with approval, since they enabled the angler to fish at the depth of his choosing.

The Colonel had always tied his own flies. In many ways he regretted the passing of those exotic feathered creations - Jock Scott, Green Highlander, Silver Doctor, Beauly Snowfly, and many others - but admitted they had been the devil to tie, with their component parts and built wings. The more recent hair wings, tubes and Esmond Drury hooks had made things much simpler.

He feared for the future of salmo salar, citing sea and estuarine netting, commercially orientated poaching, river pollution and water abstraction as threatening its very existence.

The onset of ulcerative dermal necrosis in the late 'sixties and early 'seventies had saddened him so much that he had stopped fishing for three years until the worst of the disease had passed.

That last season conditions were good; there had been a small spate and the river was still slightly coloured. We knew that the Colonel nursed a secret ambition - to get his thousandth salmon - and we were so confident that he would do so that we arranged for bottles of celebratory champagne to be put on ice.

The Colonel was getting quite stiff and unsteady, so we contrived to put him on the easiest beats with good shingle and to keep an eye on him. However, once past the natural hazards of muddy banks and stiles and in the water his casting was still immaculate, and if his sight was not as good as it had been he could still put a fly on a small leaf.

From the first day as the river fined down we all killed fish, except the Colonel, although he had several good sea trout and hooked two salmon which came unstuck for no obvious reason. It goes like that sometimes; the expert fishes beautifully and is clean, while the less skillful come home with fish.

On the afternoon of the penultimate day young Jane, a novice on her first salmon fishing trip, was detailed to keep a surreptitious eye on the Colonel. She took her responsibility very seriously, always keeping him in sight. She walked along to where he was fishing Elm Pool and he told her that he had risen a fish several times but it refused to take. Strange creatures, autumn salmon, he said. They sometimes took notions; they would rise without taking several times and then, quite suddenly - bang. Why didn't she see if she could do any better?

Jane was nervous about casting in the presence of a master, but he told her the exact spot under the opposite bank where the fly must land and, at her third attempt, she got it right. As the line came round in the current it halted and tightened, the rod bent and the fish was hooked. The Colonel kept to Jane's left side while she played it, encouraging her and occasionally giving her a little helpful advice. When at last the fish was tired he netted it for her. He was as delighted as she was and told her that she would catch many more salmon in her life, but would never forget her first.

The Colonel remained as cheerful as ever, but we were becoming increasingly anxious. Everyone knew about his thousandth and were all desperate for him to get it. The bailiff knew and came in every evening to enquire whether he had got his fish.

On the last day of the season I was fishing Long Pool, just upstream of where the Colonel was casting with his usual accuracy. I heard a splash and, looking downstream, saw the swirl in the water and his rod bowed. I reeled in and hurtled up the bank. Keeping well off the skyline, I watched while the Colonel played his salmon, praying that it would stay on. When it was about beaten I crept up and asked if he would like me to net it for him, an offer which he accepted gratefully. I crouched down and waited, holding my breath while he steered it skillfully into my net.

'Gently does it,' he said quietly. 'Hen fish. Red. Gravid.'

He told me to hold the net firmly, with the rim just out of the water. He put his rod down, wetted his hands and bent over the fish. Holding her in the submerged folds of the net he gently removed the fly - all the time talking as if to calm her: 'What's a mature lady like you doing getting caught? Surely you must have seen an artificial fly before?'

He removed her from the net and held her lightly in the water with her nose facing the current, until she had regained her equilibrium. 'You'll be all right in a moment,' he said. 'It's the last day of the fishing season, so you should be safe enough now. All you've got to do is find yourself a nice husband.'

Finally the fish swam out of his hands, slowly at first, then with a flick of her tail she was gone.

I could have wept as I watched her go. I don't know if it was relief for the salmon or pity for the Colonel, or a combination of both. By that time it was quite late in the afternoon and we packed our things and made our way back across the field to the car.

There was a salmon on the hall ashet when we arrived back, a nice clean, fresh-run fish taken from Bridge Pool. We drank the champagne that evening because, in our opinion, the Colonel had landed his thousandth, but we knew that he would not be entering that fish in his game book, that the tally still stood at 999 and probably always would.

The bailiff called, and when I told him what had happened he declared that the Colonel was a proper angler, a real gentleman, one of the old school, and that there were not many like him these days.

We did not see the Colonel again. However, the following spring we received a note from him. He had gone to fish the Wye, had tottered - his word - down to the river on the first morning after breakfast and, practically first cast, was into a salmon. It was a fine fresh-run fish of 15 pounds with sea-lice, which the ghillie had netted for him. It had been duly entered in his game book. A nice round thousandth.

Soon afterwards the Colonel's obituary appeared in The Times. After all the usual details of background and his outstanding war record, there was noted the fact that he had been a passionate and skilled salmon angler. I think he would have liked that.

Night fishing for Sea Trout

Dog days, when "The small birds will not sing aloud, The springing trout lies still'. Not the most auspicious time for a week's fishing holiday, but better by far to spend it on a river bank than sweltering in the city. Never before having attempted to fish in such conditions, I was surprised to find that they could be turned to advantage.

First of all we walked the water, and what a metamorphosis there had been since spring. Now the banks were overgrown, and in low water the skeleton of the river bed was revealed. Here was a shelf, only previously guessed at, where salmon could lie, oblivious to any lure. There, rocks that constituted an invisible snag in higher water. Secrets now exposed were stored in memory against the time that they would be hidden again, submerged, deep under water.

Then James told me about night fishing for sea trout, which had been his objective all along. I had a lot to learn. He taught me how to select and reconnoitre the pool to be fished, choosing a nice long pool ending in a shallow tail. It had an easy shingle beach from which I could fish, and good wading for him a little upstream. There was neither high bank nor tree to hinder a back-cast.

In daylight I was instructed to stand at a pre-selected spot and to cast down the pool, first in the ordinary way and then with my eyes closed. "You'll lose your rhythm in the dark at first," he said, "but don't worry, you'll soon get used to it."

So that I would know exactly how much line I had out, James made me cast a comfortable length; he then marked the spot where I held the line with my left hand with a piece of wool, fixed with fly varnish.

The whole thing seemed extraordinarily difficult to me. Wouldn't it be a good idea, I asked, for him to fish and for me to act as gillie? No, it would not. I was to experience for myself the excitement of hearing the splash of sea trout in the pool, of casting a fly into the dark, the tug on the line - often just a pluck, sometimes a hard and determined take and sometimes a gentle touch as though a leaf had stopped the fly's progress. There would also be anxiety when a fish was actually hooked, since sea trout have such soft mouths that they often escape, as many as three out of five shed the hook and are lost.

He showed me the correct way to fix my net so that it could be released quickly and easily - sea trout wait for no man to fumble around with his tackle - and a pencil torch was strapped to its handle. The tiny beam of light seemed to me to be woefully inadequate, but I was informed in no uncertain terms that I was not to be seen or heard in the pool at night.

Like salmon, fresh run sea trout do not feed regularly in fresh water. What we had to do, therefore, was to present them with reminders of the small fish on which they had fed recently in the sea. Our flies, passing them in the darkness - silver bodies, dark wings, tied spare - were intended to excite the memory of past delicacies. James intended to use an intermediate fly line with a large, but slim, lure. He gave me a floating line with a Silver Doctor tied on a No 10 Esmond Drury hook. Standing on my shingle bank, I would be able to beach most of my catch, but James had brought a strong bag, which he proposed to hang around his neck so that he could put his fish away safely without coming out of the water. And so, as far as tackle was concerned, we were fully prepared. Of course, our pockets contained the usual fly boxes, casts, priests and insect repellent (most important at night, when it is quite possible to be almost eaten alive on a river bank).

I was not a bit sure I liked the sound of night fishing. We were not going to stay out all night, were we? Sensing mutiny, James hastened to assure me that we were not. We would only be pursuing salmo trutto from dusk until midnight - or until a mist came down.

The 'Angler's Rest' is a small, very old inn with low ceilings, oak beams and inglenooks. Apart from the main building, there is a fine rod-room of a more modern construction, and over that there is a comfortable suite which is usually inhabited by the more noctambulant fishermen, and it was here that we were ensconced.

The only other fishermen in quest of sea trout were a father and his fourteen year old son. Once they had established that we only intended to stay out until midnight they no longer regarded us as serious anglers. They planned to stay out all night. The son said (and how familiar we became with this preface by the end of the week), "My father says... that you can't say you've fished for sea trout at night if you come home before dawn." And, "My father says... we have to take several rods, to cover any eventuality." In fact, between them they took five rods, loaded with different lines and lures, two huge bags of tackle, flasks of coffee and packets of sandwiches. Since we were the only people fishing by night and there was plenty of water, we had selected beats well out of each other's way.

On the first night I had one small sea trout and various incidents, but found some aspects of night fishing rather disconcerting, not least of all bats flying round my head as dusk fell - the signal to start casting. I also realised what loss of rhythm in the darkness meant. I could hear James a little upstream of me having rather more activity, his reel screeching from time to time. A mist rolled down the pool at about eleven o-clock and he waded out of the water. "We might as well stop for tonight. They've gone down for the moment." He had five nice 'peal' ranging from $1\frac{1}{2}$ to 4 pounds.

Summer night mists are strange things, hovering a few feet above ground so that one feels disembodied, unable to see what is underfoot - like slumbering bullocks. As we made our way over the field to our car we picked our way very carefully; fortunately it is possible to smell the beasts from some distance, since they object to having fishermen tripping over their prostrate bodies.

We established a very pleasant routine, fishing after dinner for three or four hours, then returning to the flat above the rod room and our creature comforts. In the morning we had a leisurely, late breakfast, after which we drove to Saunton Sands, where we played a round of golf, starting at lunch-time when most other people were off the course. After tea at the golf club, we meandered back to the 'Angler's Rest' for dinner. By the end of the week we were relaxed, suntanned and in possession of a goodly number of sea trout. Plus James' salmon. One night it was cloudy and getting dark earlier. Just as we arrived on the bank in fading light we heard a great splash in the neck of the pool. "Salmon," said James. He put on a stronger cast and went in pursuit. On about the fourth cast the fish was hooked: he tried to persuade it to surrender before it got too dark to see, but it was stubborn and took at least twenty minutes to come to the net, when the little torch proved its worth. A nice little summer fish, it weighed 9 pounds. This trophy was hung well away from any predators and we resumed sea trout fishing.

It does not take long to build a set of movements into the muscle memory, and by the end of that week I was casting in the dark as if I had been doing it all my life. I was amazed that the same pool yielded perhaps ten or twelve sea trout each night, but James said that fresh fish run up into the big sheltered pools even in very low water.

Father and son had also fished assiduously. They had persevered with their all-night sorties up and down their beats and they felt they had approached sea trout fishing intelligently and scientifically, although there was a certain reticence as to the number of sea trout hooked after midnight until around dawn. However, they had rested in the fishing hut, lighted by candles; they had consumed their night rations and together had experienced that awful 3am feeling when life is at its lowest ebb. No doubt they felt they had shared a unique experience. They also looked terribly tired and declared that they would need another week to recover from shortage of sleep.

As we left after breakfast on Sunday morning, Tom, the landlord, eyes twinkling with amusement, said the boy had confided his surprise to him. "My father says," he had said solemnly, "that the Armstrongs were extremely lucky to have caught so many sea trout and a salmon. After all, they were very poorly equipped, only one rod each and no tackle bags or anything, and they didn't stay out very long. Very lucky."

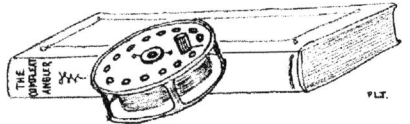

Sea Trout by day

When I consider how much preparation and forward planning goes into our fishing trips, it seems strange that the most enjoyable and productive have often been those of a more impromptu nature.

Take, for example, the year we were so busy that we decided we should remain in London to clear a backlog. We had had our early spring fishing, we told ourselves, so surely we could, just this once, forego our customary summer visit to the West Country.

By July James was beginning to look strained and wistful; weather forecasts were pretty gloomy, with rain sweeping across the South West.

"The Taw will be in spate," he said. "Sea trout will be running up, and when it fines down they'll have some grand sport at the 'Angler's Rest'."

Is it possible for telepathic messages to travel two hundred miles or more? I don't know, but I do remember James' face when he came back from answering the the telephone.

"That was Tom (the landlord of the 'Angler's Rest'). "He says he's got a room for us if we can get away. The river's up but it's stopped raining there now and the water should be perfect in two days."

We had exactly thirty-six hours in which to get ready, and before dawn on Monday we set out, arriving in time for breakfast and a full day on the river.

The water was very coloured - not the awful milk chocolate colour and raging torrent of a spring spate, but certainly far from clear. In those days, before the River Board banned anything but fly after the end of April, certain local rules obtained at the inn. At the discretion of the landlord we could spin if conditions warranted it, which they certainly did, although James decided to persevere with a sunk fly. On that first day I had two nice 'school peal' of about 1.5 pounds, fishing with a No 4 silver Mepps, and James had a rather larger sea trout on a Silver Doctor.

"If it doesn't rain any more, this could get quite exciting,' he said enthusiastically.

A recently-married young couple staying at the inn reminded us so much of ourselves years before, although the wife was much better prepared than I had been in that she had taken casting lessons before being thrown in, almost literally, at the deep end. Since we four were the only people fishing that water we fell into conversation on the first evening after dinner. It appeared that Ned and Pippa had caught nothing that day; since they did not know the river, and since it was going to be necessary to tuck ourselves into quiet backwaters at that height and colour, we agreed to share our beats and to show them the water. James explained that it was an excellent river for sea trout, which came in from the end of June, that he usually fished for them at night when the water was low but that in these conditions it was possible to have good fishing during the day.

We all have our little idiosyncrasies. Pippa was adamant that she had been taught to cast a spinner as well as a fly and that she hated being watched. She was, she said, much too self conscious to have an audience, so would we please all go away and leave her. Having put her in a nice easy place with a flat bank and some fifty yards of quite deep, comparatively snagless water we felt that she could not get into much trouble. Ned made sure she had enough baits, that her net was tied on with a quick release knot and that the clutch on her reel was at the correct tension. He then set off upstream and James and I went in the opposite direction.

By mid-morning we had had plenty of excitement, getting plucks quite consistently, hooking fish which splashed off, as sea trout will, and we had a brace each when we set out for the hut, where we had arranged to meet for lunch. On the way we came upon Pippa, sitting head in hands on the bank, the very picture of despair. On close questioning it appeared that she had hooked several fish, one of which had almost certainly been a small salmon since she had seen it jump before it disappeared with her bait and a long length of nylon, as had everything else she had hooked. She said she must be doing something terribly wrong, or the nylon must be rotten, although she had pulled it hard and it had not broken. She had started out with a dozen baits and 150 metres of 10 pound nylon on the reel: her supply of ammunition was reduced to two and the reel was almost empty.

James and Ned both tested the nylon, which they proclaimed to be perfectly all right. They then examined the rod minutely - an absolutely new, expensive rod, purchased at a famous London emporium and never used before - only to find that the agate lining of the top ring had a fracture, one end of which stuck out in a tiny, razor-sharp spike which had cut the nylon every time Pippa had hooked a fish or a snag.

The fact that we all had sea trout only added insult to injury and Pippa was inconsolable. Fortunately James always packs spare equipment, since nothing is more frustrating than to have to interrupt fishing to go for replacements in case of accident. With James' second-best spinning rod, the reel re-loaded with strong nylon and her stock of baits replenished, Pippa went forth into the same place - alone - with the light of battle in her eyes. She had worried about the fish swimming about with baits in their mouths, until we assured her that they would rub them out easily, particularly the sea trout, who have soft mouths and are adept at ridding themselves of hooks.

By the end of the day we had a nice basket of sea trout between us, Pippa having hooked and landed two herself. James was still persevering with a fly rod, although it did limit the amount of water he could cover at that height when wading was perilous.

Conditions could not have been more perfect. There was just enough overnight rain to keep the river up and coloured, and the days were fine without being too bright.

On our third day James really put a cat among the pigeons by landing a nice little 7 pound salmon. Certainly it was gratifying to know that the flood had probably brought a run of summer salmon as well as sea trout, but the thought of salmon has the same effect on some anglers as gold has on prospectors. I think I prefer sea trout, both to fish for and to eat, but the others contracted acute salmon fever. With only three days left, Ned, James and I had salmon, all around the 7 to 8 pound mark. Pippa had caught several sea trout, but Ned was determined that she was going to catch her first salmon, even if it meant staying out until darkness fell to do so.

On Friday evening we were chatting with Tom, the landlord, over pre-prandial drinks in the residents bar when we heard a car arrive. The door was flung open and in burst Ned and Pippa, dripping wet, covered with mud and glowing with triumph. Pippa was clutching a beautiful silver salmon in her arms.

We rushed to congratulate them, admired the fish and urged them to go and get dry before they told us all about it. We wrested the salmon from Pippa and promised to wash it, display it prominently on the ashet in the hall and to print her name in large letters on the attached label.

On the way out, Ned had a quick, surreptitious word with Tom and when they re-appeared, in a surprisingly short time, Tom produced bottles of champagne that Ned had ordered to celebrate Pippa's first salmon.

Over the first two bottles, with Tom and his wife joining in the festivities, the tale unfolded.

Apparently she had hooked her fish in an easy enough place, but it had turned downstream and had kept going for the sea. Ned had exhorted her to run after it, and she had, until she ran out of bank and had to take to the water. In his excitement Ned dropped his net, and then his tailer, but was unable to stop to retrieve them. Two pools downstream both the fish and Pippa were exhausted. Ned tried to hand-tail the salmon, but it slipped out of his grasp. Spurred on by Pippa's screams, he fell upon it in the shallows, scooped it up in his arms and made the safety of the bank. And there it was, and wasn't she wonderful? We could only agree.

Tom was called upon to do the honours with a further two bottles, and dinner that night was somewhat later than usual, but no one seemed to mind.

Determined to wring the last drop out of our holiday, we decided to fish all day on Sunday instead of making for London after breakfast as we usually did. We had a light, quick dinner after another blissful day on the river and set off for home, as happy and contented as it is possible to be.

It was a mistake, and I shall never be persuaded to do that again. Beguiled by the prospect of an extra day, I really had not thought the thing through. We arrived home in the small hours, extremely tired. Usually, even if it does seem to be tempting Providence, I clear the freezer to accommodate anything we might catch, but because of our hurried departure I had failed to do this. Between us we had three small salmon - which of course took priority over everything else, packets of vegetables and loaves of bread being sacrificed to house them in the deep freeze. We also had some twenty sea trout. James, longing for bed and oblivion, suggested that I put them in sinks of cold water and defer the problem until morning.

Soon after daybreak I went to the kitchen to make a life restoring pot of tea, to be confronted with the mass of thawed fish. It was not the most attractive sight. Clearly something had to be done, urgently.

Once James had departed to his work I spent the morning ringing various friends and neighbours. Having established that they would be at home and that they would be delighted to receive some splendid sea trout, I broke it to them, as gently as possible, that the fish had to be cleaned and cooked forthwith. Ever since then my offers of fish have been met with suspicion in some quarters. "How lovely," they say guardedly. "But they don't need cooking this moment, do they?"

Hypothermia

Our forebears would have considered the modern angler soft and effete. Those much tougher and more stoical men fished without the advantages of waxed cotton jackets and waterproof waders - not to mention the luxury of calor gas stoves in fishing huts. A hundred years ago would have seen them clad in heavy tweed jackets and trousers; their boots, usually hobnailed, were of stout leather, worn over thick woollen stockings.

A book published in the last century gives details of the essentials of wading in snow water in early spring. It states that on entering the river it will at first feel very cold, but after ten minutes or so this will give way to numbness. It advises the angler to come out of the water at hourly intervals and examine his legs; if red or blue, it is safe to continue for another hour, but if white or grey it is necessary to stop fishing, remove the boots and stockings and to rub the feet and legs vigorously with a rough towel until feeling and colour have returned - a most painful business - before resuming wading.

In spite of all the modern innovations in clothing and equipment it is still possible to get into trouble, as James found to his cost one raw March day. Both air and water temperatures were extremely low, the river was high with water from the snow covered moors and there was a keen wind with sleet showers.

On his water there was a canal-like stretch of something over a quarter of a mile which ran between two good pools. The banks were bare and sheer, the water deep and slow flowing. It was quite featureless, but near the middle an ancient tree stump stuck out some 4 ft below the level of the bank, at right angles to the river. The stump was about 6 ft long and perhaps 2 ft in diameter: when the river was low it was well above the water, but in a spate it was often submerged. It was covered with lichen and clumps of fungus and had for a long time been considered a nuisance, since if a fish was hooked above it and ran downstream against the left bank the line was bound to be fouled.Many a good fish had been lost in this way, but although it gave rise to complaint from time to time, somehow no-one had ever got round to hiring the necessary chainsaw and tractor to have it removed.

On the day in question the river was high and the stump was just submerged. James had fished the upstream pool and was making his way down The Canal - fishing more in hope than expectation,since there were no definite lies on that stretch and any encounter always came as a welcome surprise. About 30 yards above the stump he hooked a salmon, and it was obvious from the start that it was a sizeable fish. It jumped right out of the water before making downstream and there was absolutely nothing he could do to stop it. Inevitably the line went under the stump and before long James was down to his backing.

The fish stopped some 40 yards below the stump and swam from side to side in the current quite slowly. The backing went down below the obstruction, and a]though it moved freely up and downstream nothing he could do would persuade it to move sideways; it was obviously lying between two spikes which protruded from the underside of the old tree. Of course, the simple solution was to clear the line by pushing it deep into the water and then working it out round the end of the stump, thus establishing direct contact with the salmon again. However, cautious experiment quickly made it clear that the force of the current and the drag on the line was such that any attempt to do this would quickly result in a broken rod. Even when James gently immersed the tip into the water, his precious Hardy split cane rod bowed alarmingly.

While he was pondering on the situation, the two friends with whom he shared the water arrived and a solution presented itself to him in a flash. One of them possessed a very fancy wading staff, recently purchased at great price, equipped with a thumb notch at the top and a neat lead ball at the bottom. James proposed that he should discard his jacket, waistcoat and waders, give his rod to one of his friends and then walk out along the old stump, which was only just under the surface of the water, until he came to the point where the line was snagged. Here he would use the wading staff to trap the backing in the V of the thumb notch and push it deep into the river until it was clear of the snag. He would then advance to the end of the stump, taking the line with him. Here he would raise the line to the surface and then lift it high in the air, still using the staff. At this point, whoever had the rod could reel in line and follow the salmon downstream. Once below the stump all would be well and the fish could be played out in the normal way.

This plan was not well received. It was pointed out that the stump was very slippery and that James would almost certainly fall in. They were aware that he was a strong swimmer, but did not consider the conditions suitable for bathing. The owner of the wading- staff was particularly vehement in his protests; his staff, he said, did not float and he had worked out that its price could only be justified if it lasted for at least twenty years. In the case of a mishap James might escape from the river unscathed, but his wading staff would sink like a stone and be lost.

James overruled all objections. It was a good fish and he was not going to lose it if he could help it. He was wearing two pairs of socks; he would take one pair off and roll up his trouser legs. Wet feet was a small price to pay for a good salmon. As for the staff, it was the ideal implement for the job; the lead ball, which he would hold in his hand, would balance it nicely against the current when the other end was put in to the water, and the V thumb rest was ideal for trapping the line.

Ignoring their objections, he gave his rod to one of them with a stern warning not on any account to lose his fish. He stripped off all unnecessary clothing and emptied his trouser pockets and, having wrested the staff from its reluctant owner, he lowered himself down the bank until his feet were on the stump. Using the staff like an acrobat's balancing pole, he set out.

The water was icy cold and the two inches or so covering the obstruction was flowing surprisingly strongly. Moreover, the surface of the stump was without question extremely slippery. He negotiated the few feet which took him directly above the trapped line without mishap, albeit unsteadily, and called to the holder of the rod to bring the line to the surface. That done, he secured it in the thumb notch of the staff and pushed it deep into the river.

So far so good, but freeing the line proved not to be quite as easy as he had anticipated. The strength of the current made the wading staff difficult to control and the line did not seem to want to come free. However, by resting the staff against the upstream side of the stump and using the weight of the lead ball to help provide downward pressure, he suddenly felt the line move deeper into the water, and the whole weight of some 40 yards of line and backing, and a large salmon, suddenly came on to the end of the staff.

The unexpected pressure was almost his undoing; he wobbled violently and only saved himself by dropping down on his hands and knees. He clung desperately to the staff. and when he had recovered a measure of equilibrium he crept slowly out to the end. Here he settled astride the stump and used both hands to push the line well out into the current, urging his friend with the rod to hold it as high in the air as he could. Suddenly the line came free from the thumb notch and sprang into the air, almost sweeping James away as it did so. The custodian of the rod rushed downstream below the stump, reeling in frantically as he went, and at last was again in direct touch with the fish.

The problem of the salmon may have been solved, but the same could not be said of James. He found himself sitting astride a very slippery stump covered by icy and fast flowing water. He was now some 6 ft from the bank and facing out into the river. Also, he was clutching a heavy wading staff which, having served its purpose, was definitely excess baggage. The position was further complicated by the fact that the owner of this prized piece of equipment was dancing frenziedly on the bank above him and wailing like a banshee.

His first thought was that it would be easier if he could turn and face the bank before starting the return journey, but tentative attempts to do so quickly convinced him that this was not on, the trouble being that if he put either foot too deeply into the water the current was so strong that he would be unseated. He settled down to shuffle backwards, inch by laborious inch, towards safety, dragging the wretched staff with him. After five minutes or so he was within a couple of feet of the bank, and although he could no longer feel either his feet or his bottom the battle appeared won.

The anxious owner of the staff insisted that now James was within reach he should pass it over his shoulder and up to him. Only too glad to be rid of the thing, James shoved it backwards over his left shoulder with his right hand. The owner lay face down with his head and arms over the bank edge, ready to grab his treasure, but as James could not see the staff behind him it required some minutes of instruction and manoeuvring before it came within his grasp. At last it did and he grabbed it, crying "I've got it. Let go." James was unable to let go quickly enough and the subsequent jerk was too much for him on his precarious perch. With a despairing cry he toppled over and fell into the river on the downstream side of the stump.

Describing his sensations afterwards, James said that he was not particularly alarmed - in spite of the fact that the water was colder than anything he had ever experienced before - after all, he had fallen in or had gone in after fish on many occasions. He turned on his back in the approved manner, pointed his feet downstream and, keeping his arms well under and his head well back, let the current carry him towards a nice shingle beach which he knew was only a hundred yards downstream. The initial shock of the icy water took his breath away, but soon he began to feel quite comfortable, even warm. The strangest thing was that he stopped worrying or even thinking about anything; it was like being in a dream. The first thing he remembered after that was his annoyance at his friends, who dragged him out of the river with considerable difficulty. He resented the interference and wanted only to go on drifting peacefully.

While this was James' version of events, his friends had reason to take a much more serious view of the situation, although neither of them had been immediately aware of any danger. The one with the rod had worked his way quickly downstream below the fish, which was already tiring from its struggles, played it out and beached it on the shingle below the Canal. Having used the priest and stowed the salmon safely up the bank, he hurried back upstream and arrived just in time to see James topple off the stump. He joined the third member of the party, now happily reunited with his wading staff, and the pair of them watched James swim out into the current, turn on his back and float downstream, feet first, in the manner recommended by the pundits.

Neither was unduly concerned. They had seen him swim in the river several times before without difficulty, so they walked along the bank, keeping pace with him and making ribald comments, particularly stressing their opinion that the Lady of Shalott and Ophelia had done this sort of thing very much more artistically.

In due course James reached the shallows opposite the shingle, and they advanced to the river's edge, expecting him to turn over and swim to the shore, where they were ready to give him a hand to dry land. When he made no effort to do any such thing, but continued to float downstream, they first called to him, thinking that he had misjudged his landing place. Finally, realising that he would soon be through the shallows and out of easy reach, they waded rapidly into the water, grabbed his arms and dragged him out. When his reaction to this act of mercy was merely mild and slightly somnolent annoyance it became clear to his friends, both of whom were doctors, that all was not well. They arrived at the same conclusion immediately; the conditions were such that James was suffering from hypothermia.

One of them owned a luxurious caravan, which he kept on a small hill overlooking the river and which he used when he went fishing. This was only a few hundred yards away and, seizing James by the arms, they half carried and half trotted him towards this haven, ignoring his feeble protests. When they reached the caravan they turned the calor stove up to its maximum, stripped off his wet clothes and proceeded to rub him down vigorously. They commented afterwards on the strange colour changes which took place during this process. At first he tended to a greyish-white, most marked in his arms and legs; this changed to a mottled purple which gradually faded through various shades of blue to red, which eventually subsided to a dusky pink.

His demeanour also changed. At first he was lethargic and uninterested in his surroundings, but then began to shiver violently. Next he complained of severe pain in his hands and feet as feeling returned. Eventually these symptoms passed off and his mental state returned to normal.

After consuming three cups of hot and heavily sweetened tea he was put to bed, well wrapped in blankets. The owner of the caravan rather sheepishly produced two rubber hot water bottles, which were tucked into his cocoon, and within minutes he was sleeping soundly. That evening he awoke and got up none the worse for the experience: he borrowed some clothes from his friend and returned to the hotel in time to consume a hearty dinner.

The fishing holiday was completed without further incident and there were no ill effects, but on returning home James consulted all the textbooks he could find dealing with hypothermia. His only subsequent comment was that his experience had convinced him that it must be one of the most peaceful ways to die.

Nearly another monument

Most British rivers have a Monument Pool, sometimes more than one. Such pools are named in remembrance of an angler who dies in the very act of playing a salmon, and subsequently his friends commemorate his dramatic departure from this life by having a stone set in the bank bearing his name. Occasionally the fish has been landed and is safely ashore before the angler succumbs, but it has been known for another fisherman to happen along, see the body and, having established that nothing more can be done for the unfortunate angler, pick up the rod, reel in line, to find a salmon still hooked. It only remains to play the fish out and, if possible, to land it.

There was very nearly another Monument Pool on one West Country river some years ago. James was fishing the top beat of his water, which abutted on the lowest beat of water which belonged to a nearby fishing lodge. A bend in the river and a stickle separated the two beats, the only boundary marker being an old notice on a tree by a stile.

He arrived on the bank, surveyed the pool, selected a fly - a Thunder and Lightning, one of his own tie - and took several minutes and a great deal of care getting into the water quietly. All was very peaceful. However, he had made no more than three casts when he thought he heard a cry from upstream. He stopped fishing and listened. It came again, fainter this time, but unmistakably a human cry and of someone in trouble. He reeled in quickly and went in search of the source of the sound.

As he rounded the bend of the river he saw an elderly gentleman sitting on the shingle bank, his rod point raised to heaven and well bent. As James got nearer he could see that he was in distress, his face grey and strained, his hands trembling. He could also see salmon splashing downstream, making for the stickle.

"Thank God," gasped the angler. "Angina. Pills in my inside pocket. Can't reach them. Can't let go of the rod."

James grabbed the rod with one hand and helped to extract the pills with the other. When he had placed one under his tongue and rested on the bank for a time, the angler began to look much better. Meanwhile James got the fish under control and walked it up into the main pool.

After a further ten minutes had elapsed the angler proclaimed himself sufficiently recovered to continue playing his fish. Certainly he was a better colour and no longer in pain, so James handed him back his rod. However, it was soon obvious that not only was the man not very fit but that he was also completely inexperienced at playing salmon, and the fish began to take command almost immediately, making its way downstream again.

The strain was too much, and again he had to give James the rod while he sat down and took another pill. Once more James walked the fish upstream, and was preparing his tailer with a view to landing it when the angler staggered to his feet.

"Please," he said. "It's my very first salmon and I would like to land it myself even if it kills me."

James thought it might very well do just that, but decided not to argue against such determination. After all, there are worse ways to go. Fortunately it was not a large fish; seeing it swirl in the water, James estimated it to be about 10 pounds, but it was certainly not tired yet. Twice more he had to take the rod while the angler sat down to rest on the bank.

At last the fish was beaten, and he coaxed it into shallow water near the bank, where it lay on its side. He made sure the angler was ready, handed him the rod and told him to keep a steady strain on the fish. James then waded into the water and tailed the exhausted salmon by hand, bore him ashore and administered the last rites.

"Well done, Sir," said James, with considerable relief. "Fine fresh fish, about 10 pounds."

He had practically to prize the rod out of the anglers hands, since he stood still clutching it grimly.

The ordeal over, the two sat admiring the fish. The angler agreed with James that perhaps he had had enough excitement for one morning and that he should now return to the lodge.

They made their way back slowly, James carrying the fish, rods, net and tackle bags. On arrival, the angler invited James in for a drink, insisting that he was now quite recovered and that a large whisky would see him fully restored.

"My doctor says it's good for the circulation," he said with a smile.

Over the drinks he confided that it was entirely due to his doctor that he had taken up fishing. He was head of the family firm and had not missed a day's work since he started as a teenager. At the age of seventy he had consulted his doctor about pains in his chest, and had been given some pills and some advice. He was to take things easy, to let the young men do the work. Now that he was into injury time, as it were, he should relax, take up some hobby - something not too energetic, something peaceful. The doctor, although not an angler himself, was of the opinion that fishing might do admirably.

He had taken the doctor's advice, and, never one to do things by halves, had visited a famous London firm where he had arranged a course of casting lessons, had been fitted out with all the necessary equipment and, on their advice, had booked into the fishing lodge where they assured him, quite correctly, the salmon fishing was pleasant and easy.

James, who could think of nothing more likely to produce palpitations in even the healthiest heart than the hooking and playing of a salmon, particularly by a complete novice, did his best to explain things gently to the old man. He said that he himself had fished all his life and had caught a good many salmon, and he still believed it to be the ultimate experience in sporting excitement, and certainly it was not always peaceful. He made his new acquaintance promise never in future to fish alone, but always to go with a friend, or better still a gillie, because his next salmon, and the next, and the next, would be just as thrilling.

Before parting they exchanged names and addresses, and shortly after James had returned to London a case of fine claret was delivered to his rooms. The accompanying note read - "Drink to my salmon and wish me a few more. With grateful thanks.'

A day on a chalk stream

James learnt to fish, shoot, ride and play golf as a child, and he really should have known better than to marry a city girl. However, he has spared no effort to complete my education, particularly with regard to golf and fishing.

Perhaps it is a pity that my first encounters were with salmon and sea trout, because there is now no doubt at all in my mind that fishermen brought up on smaller quarry, and from an early age, have a much better grounding in all aspects of river lore. I had fished for trout both in river and lake and I thought I knew about game fishing, but I was to find that I had still an awful lot to learn.

One Sunday evening in early May, James answered the telephone and came back, eyes gleaming. "That was Bill. He's invited us over for a day's fishing on Wednesday".

"Lovely," I said, for a day spent on a river with our old friend is pure joy. A large, gentle man, Bill knows a great deal about a great many things - birds, music, art, golf, fishing - and time spent in his company goes very quickly. His life has spanned more than eight decades and has never been short of action. He had recently acquired a beat on one of the famous chalk streams from a friend who, sadly, could no longer fish.

I thought I was quite competent to fish a fly on any water, but James warned me that I would find chalk stream fishing rather different from anything I had previously encountered; one had to put the fly down on a sixpence and it must land, as was remarked in rather different circumstances, 'Like a butterfly with sore feet' He suggested that I had better go and practice on the lawn.

"About flies," said James. "Of course Bill's a purist. Dry fly only, on barbless hooks." He handed me a beautifully illustrated book by John Goddard, the entomologist. "It's all in there. The section on 'Ephemeroptera' is the one you want."

James disappeared into our rod-cum-gun-cum-golf club closet to select suitable rods from his very large and varied collection, while I became engrossed in the life cycle of upwinged flies (egg, nymph, sub imago or dun, imago or spinner).

It is quite a romantic and tragic little story. The eggs laid in the water by the female spinner sink to the bottom, where, in a matter of days, they hatch into nymphs. In this form they take refuge under stones and in weed, moulting from time to time as they grow. Depending on various circumstances, it may be many months before the adult nymph ascends to the surface, sheds its shuck and sits on the water drying its wings. Now it is at its most vulnerable, as trout feed avidly on the emerging and floating duns before they can fly. Trout are also in some danger at this stage, since all the skill of the fly-tyer's art and all the delicacy of the angler's casting are aimed at making the artificial fly look and behave like the natural insect. Once safely airborne, the dun sheds its final skin and emerges as the spinner, with shining gossamer wings, glistening body and graceful tails. After a spectacular aerial ballet, in which the spinners mate, the female lays her eggs on the water and, sadly, dies. It is comforting to know that the male, almost as ephemeral, does not outlive her by many hours.

James appeared bearing two rods which he thought would be suitable for our purpose. For me there was an 8 ft Hardy 'Casting Club de France', which was probably somewhat older than I, and for him there was a 9ft Hardy 'Phantom", which had also seen much active service. Who knows how long he had had them, or where they had come from? It does not do to enquire too closely into a husband's treasured possessions, lovingly accumulated over many years.

"I'll have to tie-up some special casts," he said. "Bill won't be fishing anything stronger than 3X nylon."

From a vast collection of dry flies James chose a few patterns he thought would be appropriate - upwinged olive duns, blue duns, which were really a lovely smokey grey, and some Greenwell's Glorys. He also produced some drab little flies ringed with copper wire, which he called Sawyer's nymphs.

"I know you are always careful getting into the water, and I know you don't go splashing about," said James, "but this is different. You don't wade and you must be invisible on the banks of a chalk stream; it's more like stalking really. The fish mustn't see you."

It all sounded very complicated to me and I was becoming apprehensive and afraid of disgracing myself.

Wednesday dawned fine and bright, a good to be alive day. May in England, and on a river bank with close friends - idyllic. Bill checked our tackle, nodding his approval at the small rods, James' choice of flies - to which Bill added one or two of his own tie - the size 16 hooks and the fine nylon casts.

The first thing which struck me was the clarity of the water. In fact, walking through a small feeder stream I miscalculated completely, thinking it was shallow but finding that it came to the top of my boot.

James was dispatched off upstream, since he came into the 'skilled' category, and Bill undertook his favourite role as coach and gillie to the initiate.

"Always look first," he advised. "You must know where the fish are, which fish are feeding and what they're feeding on."

To my amazement it was possible to see the gravel on the bottom of the river, beds of weed streaming in the current and fish lying with only their tails waving lazily. I looked around to see how much room I had for a backcast and found that there was precious little. James had been quite right, this was going to take rather more finesse than I had previously required, or probably possessed.

Before long there were one or two tell-tale rings on the surface of the stream. "Ah, good," said Bill. "The rise is just beginning. They're olive duns, you've got the right fly on already." He pointed. 'Look, here they come."

Sure enough, there were little upwinged flies drifting down the river like a flotilla of tiny ships in full sail.

Bill selected one trout, now feeding quite steadily, which could be seen lying just under the surface. "Cast upstream of him and let your fly float down past his nose and he'll probably take it."

In my anxiety to get it right first time I succeeded in landing my fly with a 'plop' right over the trout's nose. The object of my endeavours gave one flick with his tail and made for a nearby patch of weed, where no doubt he decided to complete his interrupted breakfast sub-surface on ascending nymphs.

I was embarrassed, but Bill was very patient. "Never mind," he said. "Let's find another in an easier place."

My second effort was, I thought, several hundred per cent better, but Bill said my fly was dragging, the current having caught the line. Certainly the fly seemed to be leaving a small wake, and it continued its course unmolested. I was mildly irritated at my ineptitude and the unexpected difficulties of the whole project and I asked Bill to show me how it should be done. He proceeded to give an immaculate demonstration of what separates the expert from the novice. His fly went out upstream, landed gently on the water and drifted neatly down over the trout's nose. The fish took it lazily, turning down, and I thought he had missed it because it seemed ages before he tightened his line.

"Got him," he said.

It was a lovely brownie, about 1.5 pounds, which at least I managed to net efficiently, bearing in mind Bill's barbless hooks. I was surprised how easily the trout came to the net.

"No point in playing them for longer than necessary," he said. "Sooner they're back in the water the less damage is done," and with this, he dipped his hand into the river, deftly removed the hook and then held the fish in the current until it had regained its equilibrium and swam out of his fingers.

I asked if he kept any of his fish. "Yes, I usually take a brace home, but the smaller ones go back to do a bit of growing. No point in taking more fish than you need. Now you try again."

I continued to cast during the morning rise and rose one, but made the mistake of tightening too soon; the hook came away and the fish splashed off.

"You must give it time to take the fly and turn away," said Bill. "No need to strike, just count to three and raise the rod point."

The fish ceased feeding and the rise was over for the moment. James appeared looking pleased with himself, carrying a nice brace of beautifully marked trout, brown with red spots on their plump sides.

"Lovely condition, Bill. Nice hatch of fly this morning."

During lunch we sat and watched the river, Bill pointing to seemingly impossible places where he had taken trout. "A 3 pounder from under that bush." And "I had a rare battle with a big one $4\frac{1}{2}$ pounds - when he got into the weed over there."

From time to time we were delighted to see flashes of electric blue as kingfishers sped up and down the river.

We waited patiently for signs of the next rise, and during this slack period James asked Bill if he could try a few casts with an upstream nymph, showing him what he proposed to use.

"Ah, a Sawyer," said Bill. "Don't care for them much myself, but some people like using them. By all means try it."

James crept to the river's edge and located a likely trout, holding his station between weed beds. He cast the nymph up and across, bringing it down over the fish, who took no notice at all. Muttering something about "Not deep enough and not far enough in front," he cast again. This time we actually saw the fish open its mouth, the white lining showing clearly, and James tightened quickly, hooking it firmly in the scissors. It proved to be a nice 3 pound brownie and it was duly knocked on the head.

"That'll do," said James. "We'll wait for another rise, but I'm very fond of the upstream nymph myself. Very useful when there's no hatch."

During the afternoon we were rewarded with another good hatch of rather darker olive duns and the fish began feeding again. I urged Bill to give another demonstration, which he did, giving a masterly performance, casting with unerring accuracy.

"Never take your eye off the fly," he said. "Concentration and vigilance is required for this sort of fishing. It simply isn't possible to think of anything else when you're casting to a rising fish."

Within ten minutes he had landed another splendid 2 pounder, which he killed. He then insisted that I should try again.

By the time the rise was over I had hooked three trout, returning two and killing one. I had missed several because of what James called 'pre-ignition', which apparently meant that I tightened too soon snatching the fly out of the fish's mouth.

When the rise ended we had tea and prepared for our long drive home. We thanked Bill for a marvellous day. "Now you must come over and try our lake for rainbows, said James. "But there's nothing quite like a good chalk stream, that's proper fishing."

I agreed with him wholeheartedly. The day had certainly taught me a few lessons, and not only about fishing. I decided in future not to assume that I could do something well before watching an expert at work.

Lake Rainbow

Rainbows are wonderful - in the right setting. Of course I refer to the scaled and finned variety, salmo gairdneri. But in the wrong places, notably rivers, they can become a menace. Great wanderers, they travel long distances to places where they are unwelcome; having voracious appetites, they grow very quickly and consume more than their fair share of the larder, to the detriment of indigenous fish.

On the other hand, in their proper place, in the still waters of lakes and reservoirs, they are an unmixed blessing. Stocked fisheries are not new, but in recent years they have increased in number and popularity, which can only be a good thing since certainly there would not be room for us all on the river banks. The simultaneous increase in the numbers of fly fishermen is also beneficial, for as a breed they appreciate and protect their environment and the wildlife with which they share it.

We are extremely fortunate, James and I, to belong to a long established fly fishing club whose lakes have the most idyllic setting. They are rich in wildlife, the fish are in superb condition - pink fleshed and extremely good to eat - and there is an abundant supply of fly, shrimp, water snails and other food. The fish are predominantly rainbow and all catches are meticulously documented, the lakes being re-stocked regularly. A stream, controlled by sluice gates, runs through the lakes and stewponds.

Having had a splendid day with Bill on his chalk stream, we wanted to return his hospitality. He agreed to come to the lakes, although he professed to being dubious about fishing for rainbow from a boat. Bill, a purist, fishing only the dry fly on size 16 hooks and 3X nylon on his chalk stream, is in his high eighties. He has a most tranquil, imperturbable air whenever he fishes.

Rainbow are early risers. James and I like to be on the water and fishing by eight o'clock at the latest, which in the summer means that often when we arrive there is a mist on the lakes, shrouding the trees and banks so that they are rather like a tarn of Arthurian legend.

Bill had been told to bring a stout trout rod, a floating line and a spare spool loaded with a slow-sinking line. James had said that he would supply the casts and suitable flies. When we arrived Bill already had his rod assembled and was ready for the day. James, checking his tackle, made him discard his cast as being much too fine for the lakes and gave him a replacement which tapered to a 6 pound point.

Bill was not impressed. "Good lord, James, you could hold the Queen Mary with that."

We made him put on the slow-sinking line since it was rather early and chilly and the air was cooler than the water. "Just until it warms up a bit," said James.

When we have a visitor to the lakes I act as engine and gillie, choosing the flies, tying them on, rowing the boat and netting the fish. I selected a nice little muddler minnow on a size 12 hook for Bill. By the look on his face it was quite obvious that he had never seen one before. Later he was to tell his family and friends that the Armstrongs had made him fish with thick nylon rope and a thing that looked like a shaving brush and was called a 'nobbler'.

"You may laugh, Bill," said James, "but if you get into one of our rainbows they won't come to the net as obligingly as your chalk stream trout."

"My dear James," guffawed Bill, "this stuff would hold a spring salmon."

"Only if your name is Wanless," said James.

I anointed the flies and the casts with our own special goo made from fuller's earth and glycerine so that they would sink quickly, and we set off. James settled Bill in his swivel seat, instructed him to cast into the breeze to avoid drifting down on the fly, warned him of the dangers of casting together and told him that if one hooked a fish the other must reel in very quickly and get his rod out of the way. Bill still looked amused.

I rowed them out into the middle of the lake, put out the drogue and sat back to await events. James was the first to hook a fish; it took deep and immediately tore out line, the reel making a very happy sound. Bill calmly started to reel in his line.

"Get your line in, Bill. Quickly," said James. There was a slight increase in the pace of his retrieval. "Quickly," shouted James. "Get your line out of the water."

At this the fish turned and ran back towards us, and Bill was then able to see that James' urgent tone was justified. He just got his line clear and his rod almost stowed out of the way when the fish passed on its first tour round the boat. James took evasive action, standing up and holding his rod at arm's length above his head. The moving line missed Bill's rod-tip but failed to clear his hat, which was swept off into the water, where it set sail. Before it had gone too far I managed to net it and restore it to its owner.

"That fish must be foul-hooked," said Bill.

"Of course it isn't foul-hooked," said James. "They always behave like this. They're good fighters."

Bill looked sceptical and expressed the opinion that it must be James' method of playing the fish that made it dash about in such a fashion. In about ten minutes it tired and was drawn safely to the net. It was hooked firmly in the scissors, a very nice three pound rainbow.

"We have to kill everything we catch," James explained. "We're allowed eight fish on the day, four each, and we don't put anything back."

Before long Bill was into a fish: his reel screeched and his little trout rod was bent double. He started to play it on the reel, in spite of James' exhortations to bring in the line by hand. It was not until the trout made its run back towards us that he could see there was no way he could keep in touch with it unless he pulled in line through the rings very fast indeed. There was a strange, surprised look on Bill's face, and James winked at me.

"It must be a big one," said Bill after some fifteen minutes' hard work. At last, safely in the net it also weighed three pounds.

Gradually, as the sun became stronger and the air warmer, there were hatches of midge on the lake. House martins that had been flying high now dipped low, skimming the water, taking fly from the surface. Both James and Bill changed to floating lines and I tied them on different colours of Chironomid pupae, 'buzzers', tiny flies tied to represent hatching midges, with white tails and minute bunches of white material over the hook-eyes to imitate the breathing filaments of the naturals.

"They must sit on the surface film, Bill," said James. "If you see your line move at all, tighten, and you'll probably find a fish on. They take so gently that you have to watch closely all the time. They can take these pupae in their mouths and spit them out again without you ever knowing they have been near the fly."

Facing upwind there was no need to cast very often: the pupae, watched closely by us, drifted gently down the lake behind the boat. Bill sat. We all sat. After about ten minutes, when it appeared that nothing was going to happen, Bill took his eye off his fly and reached for his pipe. Inevitably, at that moment his fly disappeared. I saw the faintest movement of his line and cried "Tighten, Bill." He gave an involuntary jerk with his right hand and found himself into a fish.

"Bless my soul," he said.

James also had a good trout on a buzzer, and they both lost a couple of fish when their hooks came adrift. Much to James' disgust he was broken by something large which took him with a bang. Then the hatch of midges seemed to be over. James decided to try a small pink shrimp, which accounted for another good rainbow. I produced a damosel nymph for Bill, having seen a few electric-blue Zygoptera on the water. He regarded the long, slim green fly with its articulated body with distaste. I explained that its body was jointed to make it wiggle in the water. Bill sniffed, but he hooked two good trout on it. James noticed a large cinnamon sedge that had landed in the boat, so I tied one of those on for him, and within another fifteen minutes I had netted the last fish of the day.

We had lunch in the sunshine outside the lodge, watching other anglers casting, Canada geese flighting in, coots fighting in the reed beds, swans, duck, the irritating little dabchicks who can fool one into thinking that a fish is feeding, and all the myriad things that bustle and scurry about their business on the banks of a lake.

I asked Bill how he thought lake fishing for rainbow compared with his chalk stream. He was silent for a while before delivering himself of a great truth. "It's different," he said.

Losing Salmon

It can happen to anyone. At any time. Without warning. No respecter of persons, or of reputations, in its most virulent form it drives strong men to drink. Quite simply, the angler loses salmon. I don't mean that fish splash off almost as soon as they are hooked; they can be on for anything from five minutes to that moment when they are just at the net or tailer. Nor do I mean fish that are lost through obvious carelessness or unavoidable accidents, and I don't mean single fish. For no accountable reason, a perfectly competent angler will lose several, often many, consecutive salmon.

I was standing up to mid-thigh in a much-loved pool on a fine May day. Conditions could not have been more perfect; the water was a nice height and colour, there was good cloud cover, birds sang, there was an excellent run of fish, which were moving in a most encouraging way, and I thought how wonderful it was to be alive and on a river. As I started to cast at the top of the run a salmon jumped just downstream. Within a few minutes I had worked my way down over him and as the fly came round in the current I saw the boil on the surface; the line moved away and when I tightened I felt that delicious shock up the arm and the familiar tingle in the chest. He was on and this was what it was all about.

It was an easy enough place. I backed out of the river and got below the fish, holding the rod point well up. For a good ten minutes the salmon and I were engaged in the usual classic fight then, quite suddenly, the line went slack and he was gone.

It is always dispiriting to lose the first salmon of a holiday and as I pulled in line to examine the cast and fly I was certainly disappointed, but not yet in despair. The business end of my tackle was in good order; the fly was intact and the hook was just the right sharpness.

To be absolutely safe I re-tied the fly, waited for a few minutes and started down the pool again. By the time James arrived a couple of hours later I had lost two more salmon, both of which had been on for some fifteen minutes. He came along the bank carrying a fine fresh-run fish.

"Anything doing here?" he asked, and when I told him about my disastrous morning he was sympathetic but brisk, enquiring whether I had checked that the hook was all right and whether I had kept tight on the fish. I was, understandably, pretty waspish at what I, in my finely tuned mood, construed as criticism. Ignoring my tone, he said 'Poor love. Never mind. There are plenty of fish about. You're bound to land one soon."

During the afternoon I lost another fish and James had two more beauties, both about 12 pounds. When we got back to the hotel the rest of the party had fish and I was the only one clean. I had learned quite early on that in salmon fishing success is marked by gleaming silver on the ashet at the end of the day and that hard luck stories may excite superficial sympathy, but there is always the feeling that either the angler has been inept or is given to exaggeration. So I replied to enquiries with what I hoped was a carefree smile and said that I had had a few offers but that nothing had connected yet.

The second day was very much a repetition of the first. Two fish were lost, although they felt solidly hooked at the time. Everyone else had at least one salmon.

By the third day fishing was far from the joy it should have been and I came to dread hooking a salmon because I knew, with the most appalling certainty, that it was going to come unstuck. I tried everything - being gentle with one, giving it plenty of time to run; with another I gave it plenty of butt, being quite ruthless in turning it in the hope of ensuring that the hook was right home over the barbs, getting it towards the net as soon as possible - but to no avail; all were lost at some quite late stage in the proceedings. I was distraught in private and, with difficulty, sanguine in public. James knew, of course. "Just be patient," he counselled kindly. "It's obviously not your fault. You're bound to get one sooner or later. Bound to."

I thought I must have done something terrible to be thus punished by the river gods and was thinking in terms of appeasement - throwing myself in, for example. What made it worse was that no one else was in the slightest way affected by the same gremlin. Sometimes, in trout fishing, there are days when fish are pronounced to be 'coming short' and anglers in general complain that although they are moving fish consistently nothing is taking a firm hold. But on this occasion the entire party was enjoying very productive sport and only I was without fish or excuse.

On the fourth morning I was fishing, without much hope, in what had been one of my favourite spots before my now rather jaundiced views on salmon had become established. James was fishing just upstream, beyond the stickle which separated our two pools. A salmon took my Hairy Mary and the clicking of the reel turned into a veritable screech as it ran downstream. Afterwards James said he hadn't moved so fast since he won the 100 yards at school a good many years back. He reeled in, left his rod on the bank and came hurtling down to where I stood, trembling uncontrollably with excitement and fear, my rod well up and the line tight. He was at my side within seconds.

The fish jumped just once, letting us see that it was large and fresh run and quite beautiful. It appeared to me to be mocking us. I was beyond words, beyond prayer, beyond everything. Neither of us spoke; my face ached from clenched jaws and James dared not utter either advice or encouragement. After some ten minutes the fish, far from being played out and not at all tired, came towards our bank. James waded quietly into the water, tailer ready, and waited well below the fish. He waved to me to back away, which I did with the utmost caution, and the salmon drifted slowly downstream in the slacker water to where James crouched, motionless, his tailer deep in the river.

The fish arrived almost at his feet; there was a sudden great splash, the tailer was home in just the right place and 20 pounds of shining iridescence was safe. At that moment my cast, with the fly intact, fell into the water. It was out, and that fish would have been lost also had James not come to the rescue. With the salmon on the bank I stood and wept with relief. "'There," he said. "It's all right. That's broken the hex. What a glorious fish. You'll be all right now."

And so I was. That afternoon I hooked, played and landed another salmon, the fly so securely embedded in the scissors that I had to cut it out. On subsequent days two others played as self-respecting salmon should, so that by the end of the week confidence had returned.

"I didn't say anything to you at the time," said James, "but it happened to me once, only much worse. I lost thirteen in a row."

On the last evening of a memorable week we were sitting in the bar before dinner when James mentioned that I had lost eight consecutive fish at the beginning of the week. This provoked a whole series of horror stories in similar vein. One friend was of the opinion that I had suffered a very minor attack of the disease; he had gone a whole season losing one fish after another and it had been a long time before he was able to talk about it.

However, have no fear. It is not like a shank in golf - just hearing or reading about it does not produce the malady. It is definitely not infectious, although, happily, it is said to share one important characteristic with measles - once you have had it you are immune thereafter. My only advice to those yet to encounter the affliction is to grit the teeth and work through it. This particular ailment disappears as quickly as it comes. It does, I promise. I know.

The Devil's Bait

Rachel has never quite forgiven James for corrupting her husband and her eldest son.

Cuthbert and James are close friends, colleagues, and both are keen anglers. However, Cuthbert was a purist; he had a cottage on Exmoor and owned a couple of miles of water on one of the small tributaries, where he fished for brown trout, always with a dry fly, using only natural patterns in their season, tiny hooks and very fine nylon. His idea of bliss was to take home a basket of brown trout, three or four to the pound with the occasional half-pounder as a bonus. Cuthbert had taught his son, Anthony, to fish and they would go off happily together whenever an opportunity arose. At the age of eight, Anthony had become a very competent trout fisherman, and, under the watchful eye of his father, he cast a fly well.

James shared a beat on the main river with two friends, only about half-an-hour's drive from the cottage, and he had invited Cuthbert over for a day's fishing whenever they next happened to be in Devon at the same time.

In early September, the river was just fining down after a summer spate, but it was still very coloured. James, on holiday, was spinning for sea trout when Rachel, Anthony and his younger brother arrived on the bank. Cuthbert had been detained in London, but the rest of the family had motored over to see James and his fishing.

He explained to Anthony that the river was unsuitable for a fly but that sea trout quite often took a spinning bait in just that type of water. Rachel and her younger son, who did not care for fishing, went to look for blackberries, but Anthony accompanied James, who, in the course of the next hour or so, killed a couple of nice sea trout of about three pounds, which Anthony, quivering with excitement, netted for him.

When they returned to the hut for lunch, James explained the art of spinning with a fixed-spool reel, telling the boy that it was much easier than fly fishing and that anyone could learn to do it in ten minutes. Anthony's eyes glistened, and when James produced his spare rod and reel he proved an apt pupil. After a short lesson they set off and fished together: Anthony actually hooked two sea trout, which splashed off, but James consoled him, saying that sea trout had very soft mouths and that when spinning in fast water it was quite usual to lose a high proportion of fish hooked.

The family departed after tea, but Rachel promised that if Cuthbert arrived that night, she would try to get him to bring Anthony down again the next day.

The following morning the river had fined down a little, but it was still too thick for a fly. James was spinning one of the best pools, where the main river was joined by a large tributary, when Cuthbert and Anthony arrived in their fishing gear. James reeled in and clambered out of the river to greet them. Cuthbert said he understood that James had been leading his son astray and that he had been practically dragged to the river after a very abbreviated breakfast. In his opinion the water was far too coloured to make it possible to catch anything at all.

James handed his rod to Anthony. "There you are," he said. "Go carefully down the bank just here; there's a good shingle bottom. Throw the minnow well out to where the stream comes in. Show your father how wrong he is."

Anthony scrambled down the bank and into the river, the water coming dangerously near the top of his thigh waders. Remembering his lesson, he checked the tension on the reel before making a very creditable cast out to where the two waters met. His father watched these proceedings with disdain, muttering about 'damned ironmongery', when Anthony's line, which had been coming round nicely in the current, suddenly stopped.

"Have you got the bottom, Anthony?" called James, getting ready to go and get him unsnagged.

"If I have, Uncle James," replied Anthony tremulously, "the bottom's moving."

At this point the line moved briskly across the river, the reel clicking merrily.

"He's in a fish, Cuthbert, exclaimed James, and he plunged into the river to stand at Anthony's left side. "Keep the rod well up. Don't do anything if he runs away from you; be ready to reel in quickly if he starts to move towards you. I'll steady you and we'll wade downstream and try to get below him."

The pair struggled down the river, James clutching Anthony firmly by his belt, until they arrived well below the fish. In the meantime Cuthbert watched from the bank. "What is it, James? A sea trout?"

"No, I think..." At this moment a bright silver salmon jumped out of the water at the upper end of the pool.

"For God's sake, take the rod James, it's a good salmon. It's too big for him, he'll lose it."

"No," said James. "It's his fish, he hooked it, he can kill it." then to Anthony - "Keep your eye on the fish and keep the line tight. Reel in when you can, but don't rush him. I'll hang on to you, you're quite safe."

The next twenty minutes saw a great struggle. Anthony held on to his fish, James held on to Anthony and Cuthbert showered them both with unsolicited and unheeded advice from the bank. At last the fish tired and was coaxed into the shallows, where James tailed it deftly dragged it up the bank and used his priest. He then retrieved a very wet and bedraggled Anthony from the river. The boy insisted on carrying the eleven pound salmon back to the hut himself.

During lunch it became clear that Cuthbert's views on salmon fishing had undergone a radical change. In the afternoon Anthony was dispatched with the spare rod and reel - within shouting distance - and Cuthbert became the pupil. Both succeeded in catching a sea trout.

Next morning, as a matter of some urgency, Cuthbert and Anthony paid a visit to the nearest tackle shop to invest in the necessary rods, reels and baits for spinning, and, until the weekend when they all had to return to London, they fished each day with James, catching more sea trout, but still hoping for another salmon.

Of course, Cuthbert and Anthony still enjoy fishing the dry fly for brown trout, but whenever the opportunity presents itself they are off after larger quarry.

"I blame James," Rachel said to me some years later. "He spoilt fishing for Cuthbert and Anthony. They used to go off trout fishing for a few hours when the weather was right, and they used to come home when the rise was over. Now they go out at dawn and stay until dusk, in all weathers. I never know when they'll be home for meals and they come back in an awful mess, mud to the ears. That first salmon of Anthony's really was the devil's bait."

Always the big one

James and young Anthony, his godson, had a grievance. They both caught more fish than Cuthbert, Anthony's father, but Cuthbert caught the big ones. That he was a late convert from trout to salmon fishing only added insult to injury. In spring, when larger fish were running, James and Anthony might have 13 or 14 pounders, but it was Cuthbert who hooked a 20 pounder. In autumn, when the fish were smaller, James and Anthony would get 7 or 8 pounders, but Cuthbert somehow produced something in the teens.

This state of affairs finally came to a head one day in April. The river was fining down after a spate and was just right for spinning. James, expecting Cuthbert and Anthony to join him for a day's fishing on his water, had made his way down to a favourite spot where he had moved a fish the previous evening.

'The Bushes' was shunned by most fishermen, particularly as it was only about 100 yards upstream from 'Junction', the best pool on the beat. 'The Bushes' was a deep, canal-like stretch of some 50 yards, with a high bank on the side from which it was fished. At the top of the stretch there were two large bushes on the opposite bank, with branches hanging well out over the river. Salmon tended to lie close to this bank, just downstream of the bushes, and any attempt to cast to the lie from upstream was to court the loss of fly or bait. However, James had discovered that about mid-way down the stretch a narrow shelf of rock ran out into the middle of the river, ending in a natural platform about 4 ft square. Normally under water, he had found the shelf when exploring the river during a drought. By wading out carefully on to the promontory it was possible to throw a spinning bait upstream, under the bushes and against the far bank, and to bring it down quickly over the lie. An accurate cast was necessary and missed footing meant a ducking. Various people had lost their entire supply of baits trying that cast, leaving the overhanging branches festooned with lures. Several fishermen had actually fallen in and most had given it up as not worth the bother, but James loved the place and had killed quite a few fish there.

Cuthbert and Anthony arrived just as James, standing almost up to his knees in water on the platform, was tailing a nice fresh 12 pounder with sea lice. He made his way ashore, stepping gingerly along the shelf with his fish, and while they admired his catch, James said he was sure he had moved a larger salmon the evening before. He suggested that if either of them wanted to try it they were welcome.

Anthony was eager to get to Junction Pool, the scene of many triumphs, not to mention his first salmon at the age of eight. Cuthbert said he had never tried The Bushes and perhaps James would show him how to get safely into position.

It must be explained that Cuthbert on the river bank, or anywhere else for that matter, is an impressive figure, standing well over 6 ft and weighing perhaps fifteen stone. In London he is always immaculately dressed, but on a river bank he presents a very different picture. His lower half is relatively conventional - very old baggy corduroys and thigh waders, the straps of which have long since been replaced by string. For the rest, he wears an ancient tweed jacket over many layers of pullovers, a venerable cravat, and,to top everything, an antique, battered deerstalker. Sartorial inelegance is not his major eccentricity, however; like the snail he carries every thing he needs on his back. He does not believe in refinements like a rucksack or fishing bag. On the river bank he bears a strong resemblance to Lewis Carroll's White Knight. He carries the various items he considers essential slung on his considerable person, each suspended separately on it own loop of string. There is usually a tailer, a rolled-up plastic mackintosh, a large bag containing sandwiches and a thermos of fierce, corrosive curried soup, various other smaller bags filled with fishing tackle and a bottle of wine in a curious wicker contraption, which he maintains keeps its contents cool against the luncheon hour. James has tried, on occasion, to take a full inventory of the load to see if it actually contains a mousetrap or a beehive, but the sheer number of packages has defeated him. Unless about to use it, Cuthbert cannot be persuaded to divest himself of any of these items on the grounds that if they are attached to him he is less likely to lose them, a fact which past experience has confirmed to the full.

On the day in question, Cuthbert resisted the suggestion that he might discard some of his burden in view of the precarious wading on the shelf. He was shepherded out on to the platform by an anxious James, who was all the while exhorting him to remember that one false step would mean swimming in deep water, if indeed he did not sink like a stone. With Cuthbert safely in situ, James retired to the bank and sat down beside Emma. They both settled to watch proceedings with interest.

Cuthbert's first two casts caught in the bushes, but fortunately were retrieved without too much difficulty. He explained his lack of expertise by saying that he was using a new rod, purchased from a recently opened emporium in London. It was a second-hand 9 ft cane Hardy spinning rod which, in his opinion, was much better than the fibreglass poles favoured by James and Anthony. James had examined the rod while it was being assembled and, not to put too fine a point upon it, was not impressed; it had a definite 'droop', indicating years of successfull use, and he was very doubtful about its durability, in spite of its impeccable lineage.

Cuthbert's third cast landed in exactly the right spot and he had only retrieved a yard or two of line when the rod bent and he was obviously into a fish.

The first ten minutes or so were only remarkable in that nothing much happened. The fish went deep and swam back and forth quietly with no appearance of alarm. James, not the most patient of men, who expects some degree of action when he has a fish on, urged Cuthbert to greater endeavour.

"Come on Cuthbert, give him a bit of stick. You've got 18 pound nylon there - it'll stand a lot more strain."

Cuthbert applied more and more pressure until the old rod creaked and bent in an almost complete bow. The fish continued his sedate excursions up and down the pool. Every now and again he would go downstream, passing Cuthbert, until he reached the shallow stickle which separated The Bushes from

Junction Pool below. There he would turn and go upstream until he reached the upper limit of the pool, where a small waterfall lay between him and the next pool far upstream. Several times he attempted to swim up this obstruction but, urged on by James, Cuthbert increased the tension until the point of his rod was almost touching the water. After a few minutes of this, the fish would turn and make his stately way back into the main pool.

In a full half-hour the fish still had not surfaced and did not appear to have tired at all. James said the rod was too weak to apply any real strain, but Cuthbert maintained that he was into a very heavy fish indeed.

At last the unremitting pressure prevailed and the fish's progress was marked by an occasional swirl near the surface. Finally he rolled, showing an enormous back and a huge tail.

"My God, Cuthbert," whispered James. "It's a monster. He's tiring, though. Tell you what - I'll take my tailer and creep out on the shelf and you see if you can steer him in towards the bank on our side. I can see a couple of feet into the water, and if he comes within reach I'll slip the tailer on and we've got him."

After another ten minutes Cuthbert managed to steer the great fish towards the bank. James, kneeling dangerously near the edge of the shelf at Cuthbert's feet, had the tailer poised at the ready. At last the fish rolled on the surface and for the first time they had a good view of a salmon which was large enough to silence them both. Gradually the fish drifted downstream, almost to the shelf and almost on the surface. James, quick as a flash, slipped the tailer on, tightened, and he was fast.

"Get the line free, Cuthbert, in case I pull you in, and I'll drag him along the shelf."

James scrambled along the shelf, dragging the fish, clambered up the bank and, seizing the tailer in both hands, started to draw the great salmon ashore. At this point, just within sight of safety, the wire cable of the tailer, weakened with years of use, snapped, and the salmon plunged back into the river with a huge splash.

I shall not repeat here the actual exchange between Cuthbert and James, but when I tell you that Cuthbert spent some six years in the Royal Navy you can imagine that it was, to put it at its best, colourful. However, James noticed the free line curling briskly off Cuthbert's reel and shouted "Wind in. Wind in. Get in touch. I think he's still on."

"What a hope," said Cuthbert, or words to that effect, but, as he wound in, the line tightened and he and the fish were again in contact.

Somewhat upset by this episode, the fish swam up and down the pool rather more vigorously than before, the line making a swishing sound as it scythed through the water.

Emma, trained from a pup never to go into the water after a hooked fish, could stand it no longer. It seemed obvious to her that her master and his friend were unable to cope without some assistance. A particularly strong swimmer, she plunged headlong into the river and swam after the line as the fish swept majestically past.

Cuthbert easily surpassed his previous verbal effort, the burden of his message being that James should get his miserable, half-bred mongrel cur out of the river and away from his fish.

Having heard the commotion from Junction Pool downstream, Anthony appeared. At a glance he took in the sight of a large salmon swimming up and down the pool, closely followed by an excited golden retriever, and an apoplectic father clinging grimly to his rod on his insecure perch, giving tongue at the top of his voice.

"Get Emma ashore, Anthony," cried James. "She can't hear me, your father's making too much noise."

With the nimbleness of youth, Anthony crept out on the shelf, grabbed Emma by the collar as she and the fish passed, and towed her ashore, where she was tethered to a tree stump with a very stout piece of cord.

The salmon, worn out with his exertions, began to roll on the surface again and Anthony saw it in all its glory for the first time. "Gosh," he said in awe.

James told Anthony briefly and succinctly that his tailer had broken at his first attempt, that Anthony's sea-trout net was much too small for this fish and that he would take a pair of scissors and try to cut his father's tailer free from his back.

He then crept out to the fulminating Cuthbert and began to divide such loops of string as he could reach. He and Anthony retrieved the wine cooler, the lunch bag and the plastic mackintosh before they finally found the tailer, but at last it came free and was made ready for action.

Cuthbert, now past speech, clung desperately to his rod, steered the fish in, and James tailed it. With Anthony's help he dragged it along the shelf, up the bank and well ashore, where it was knocked on the head. They then helped the trembling Cuthbert to safety, where he at once revived himself from his hip flask.

The whole operation had taken well over an hour. The salmon weighed in at 34 pounds, the biggest caught on that river in living memory and a good 8 pounds larger than anything ever taken on that beat.

In view of all the circumstances and Cuthbert's very trying morning, James and Anthony agreed to break one of the unwritten laws of that water - 'Them as catches carries'. They slung the great fish on a long pole and carried it back to the fishing hut Cuthbert following up the rear, re-united with all his freight and carrying his rod, now more curved than ever.

The wicker container was opened, the bottle of wine broached and all three filled their glasses to toast the fish. Cuthbert had the last word.

"I told you it was a big one," he said. "I'd never have got it without a proper rod."

Halcyon Day

On the very last day of the trout fishing season we went to bid the lakes farewell, or at least au revoir, until the next spring. We were hoping for one last morning's fishing, one last tug on the line, one last plump trout in the net, before we settled down to spend the long winter evenings preparing for the next season. Reels would have to be stripped down, lines cleaned, fishing bags emptied, tidied and replenished, flies tied, all in eager anticipation of the forthcoming year.

Sometimes in early October we have an Indian summer, when warm, dreamy days continue and only light winds ruffle the water's surface; then it seems that game fishing is coming to an untimely end. Not so on this occasion. We arrived to find a bleak landscape - a cheerless day, the wind with a bite of north in it, the first leaves fluttering down on a lake that was choppy and uninviting. The reeds bent low in the chill breeze and there was no bird-song. Swallows and martins had long since flown south, and even the resident waterfowl - duck, coot and swan - were sheltering under the banks. I remarked that it looked far from promising. James agreed. "All we need now is a Knight at Arms, alone and palely loitering."

We were completely alone on the lake and after a couple of hours we had caught nothing; in fact there had been no offers at all, although we were fishing deep, hoping to cajole one last rainbow to take a Peter Ross or a Bloody Butcher. Drifting was frustrating; we went down the lake far too quickly, until we thought of borrowing an extra drogue from one of the unused boats. Rowing up against the stiff wind was tiring, but at least it served to warm us. Finally we let the boat ground against the lee shore and we sat, hunched in our Barbour jackets, scarves up to our ears, hats pulled well down, hands warming round beakers of hot coffee.

"Just one last drift," said James, "then we'll make for home."

We sat chatting quietly over our coffee, when James stopped talking in mid-sentence and went very still. Following his eyes,

I looked to the bow where we had left our rods leaning against the thwart. There, so close that I could have touched him, was a kingfisher, perched on one rod-tip. Speechless and immobile, we hardly dared breathe for fear of scaring him away. Against the stark grey of the water and sky his plumage shone sapphire and emerald, needing no burnishing from any sun. His throat was white and, beneath, he was the colour of warm terracotta. For some moments he sat there, his posture reminiscent of a disgruntled old man. Suddenly he launched himself into the water, disappearing in a cloud of spray. When it seemed that he would never surface again he appeared, wings making that lovely unhurried beat usually only captured on a slow-motion camera. With a minnow in his beak he made for a nearby bush, where he thrashed the small fish against a branch before swallowing it, head first. Then he was gone, a familiar flash of blue travelling like an arrow to the opposite bank.

The kingfisher is said to have magical powers to charm wind and waves to calm. It would be nice to be able to say that the day became clement and trout began to rise, but of course it was not so. However, for a short time, for our last drift of the year, it seemed not quite so cold, not quite so desolate and rather more hopeful.

We tied on new flies, James finally selecting a dreadful looking thing called, I think, a Girdle Bug, a pattern he had tied for a friend who had insisted that it was an absolute killer on the Colorado River. Basically it appeared to be bushy green and black, palmered with game cock hackle, but its main features were feelers, fore and aft, made of white elastic. He had never used it before.

Throughout the season a large trout had consistently shown, some twenty yards from the jetty, and many anglers had cast at it with no response at all. It was generally estimated to be at least 6 pounds in weight. We have fished on lakes which go in for very large trout, usually pellet-fed and sluggish, so that they play with all the excitement of a cardboard box and eat like cotton wool. On our lakes, very large fish are uncommon, but -they fight well.

We were nearing the end of the drift when James cast towards the jetty. A fish took him deep and slow and his reel clicked steadily. It was immediately obvious that he was into something rather bigger than usual and that it was going to take some time. With the greatest possible difficulty I managed to recover both drogues from the water, manoeuvre the boat beside a pier, throw the painter on the bank, leap out and secure the boat.

For a time James played it from his seat, but then it became necessary for him to disembark so that I could net his prize from the bank. With the boat rocking beneath him, he made the safety of the shore, where he was able to persuade the fish, very gradually, towards the waiting net. It took a full half hour, many heart stopping runs and a few prayers before the rainbow finally lay on the grass. It weighed 9 pounds and was, in the circumstances, far more valuable than any salmon of the same weight.

We packed up our things, took one last look at the lake and started for home with light hearts, even though it was the last day. But what a day - halcyon indeed.

The Bob Fly

From London to the West Coast of Scotland seemed to me an inordinately long way to go for three day's fishing.

"You'll love it," said James. "Nothing like it anywhere else in the world. Marvellous country. Mountains, glens, heather. Much too good an opportunity to miss."

And so we set out before dawn and headed north. As we neared our destination in the late afternoon it became clear that our timing had been less than perfect. We travelled in ever increasing rain, under leaden, weeping skies, surrounded by forbidding hills and, of course, when we arrived the river was rising fast, working itself up to a full spate.

Our host, Malcolm, an old university friend of James', was undeterred. The river was certainly out, but he had a boat on the loch, which held sea trout and salmon and it was not too far away. The flood was bound to have brought up a run of both, although he himself preferred fishing a team of small flies for its wild brown trout, about which he waxed quite lyrical.

After dinner on our first evening, James and Malcolm fell into deep discussion about rods and tackle. We had come prepared for a river and had nothing really suitable for fishing from a boat on a proper Scottish loch, which Malcolm announced with pride was quite different from the heavily stocked 'ponds' we had in the South. He was only too willing to provide us with anything we required from his vast collection of equipment. James was adamant that two people in a boat were quite enough; he would fish from the shore with his own rod and his own flies and Malcolm and I could do what we liked on the loch.

The next morning we set out in a Landrover - the 'nearby' loch being some fifteen miles away - and after negotiating bumpy, winding roads at what seemed like breakneck, spine-jarring speed it lay before us. Malcolm sighed with pleasure. "Isn't that a bonny sight?" I agreed. There was also a bonny breeze blowing, although it had stopped raining. Fortunately the boat was solid and broad-beamed and boasted an outboard motor, so I would not on this occasion be required to man an oar. Malcolm was proud of his system of drogues, which he had arranged so that he was able to drift sideways as well as downwind. He supplied me with a long rod and a fairly short cast, and I had already received a solemn lecture on the three flies I should use. On the point I had a Peter Ross and on the middle dropper a Blae and Black. However, it was the top dropper, the bob fly, and its management which apparently separated the men from the boys. It was supposed to skip on the surface from wave to wave and, although its proper manipulation could only be accomplished satisfactorily by a real Scot, he proposed to introduce me to the art. As for the fly itself, it was very much a personal choice, but he preferred his own modification of the Coch-y-bonddu, which appeared to be some sort of heather beetle. Malcolm claimed that its success on that particular water was unsurpassed.

I confessed to being rather dubious about three flies in such a stiff breeze. Would I not get them tangled? Would I not be better with just one? Malcolm would have none of this feeble talk. 'Lassie' was going to give the fish three choices, not only of fly but of depth and action. The previous evening he had given an impassioned lecture on this very subject, at which James had smiled quietly and made no comment. This morning he knew exactly what he was going to do, and with what, and Malcolm and I could sort out our differences whilst afloat.

The loch was impressive, fed by multiple small streams from the surrounding mountains, and there was one quite sizeable river flowing from it to the sea. There was what Malcolm described as 'a nice wee lop' on the water, and I thought how fortunate it was that I was a good sailor.

I assembled an eleven foot rod, fitted a slow sinking line and a cast already tied with three flies. Malcolm was similarly equipped. One pull and the outboard roared into life, and we were away. James was left ashore, clad in chest waders, and he immediately headed towards the efferent river.

The engine got us happily to the windward side of the loch, then Malcolm stopped the boat and cast out two drogues, one a large, flat wooden board adjusted by ropes at each end, and the other a bucket with a small hole in the bottom. "Just to slow us down a bit and give us a nice long drift." He was quite sure that conditions were right for trout.

It was tempting to cast as long a line as possible, but Malcolm insisted that this was quite unnecessary, about twice the length of the rod would do nicely. I was to keep the rod point well up so that the wind caught the line a little, to make the bob fly dance on the waves. The retrieve was to be as slow as possible. I was given the easy seat from which to cast; he probably felt safer if I did not have to put my line over the boat.

Malcolm was delighted to hook the first fish on his Coch-y bonddu, a plump three-quarter pound brown trout. I was beginning to feel doubtful about my efforts when, suddenly, there was a hard 'take' and my reel spun merrily.

"Sea trout. Probably on the point," exclaimed Malcolm. "Handle him carefully, he may be quite a good fish."

After several brisk runs it gave in, as sea trout will, and came to the net, a lovely silver fish of just over two pounds which had, indeed, taken the Peter Ross on the point. I was told to keep the rod well up while he netted the fish for me, and I realised why when I relaxed the tension when the fish was safely in the boat; the bob and middle dropper promptly entangled themselves in the net and I spent the next ten minutes extricating them and untangling the cast. The sea trout was stowed away in the bass and I was ready to go again - almost - except that the wretched bob fly had embedded itself in my woollen jumper, a happening that was repeated regularly during the day. Malcolm, who had to come to my rescue with a pair of scissors, was only faintly amused when I asked him if he was sure his 'special' was really a Coch-y-bonddu and not some sort of ravening moth.

By mid-day Malcolm had four brown trout and I had two, and the sea trout. My new woollen jumper, from Hardy's in a pleasing shade of Lovat green with suede patches, looked as if it had been made up to some lacy pattern never seen in any fishing catalogue.

We met James on the bank, looking very superior. He had taken two nice little salmon, both about seven pounds, and a sea trout, from the point where the loch flowed into the river - all on a Willie Gun tied on a size 8 Esmond Drury hook. Our host was pleased at James' success, but in his opinion he had not applied himself to the real treasures of the loch, the wild brown trout. With a gleam in his eye, which I knew of old, James said that he would now fish for trout and ignore the salmon. He firmly refused to come in the boat, preferring to remain on the bank.

When questioned, Malcolm admitted that perhaps I was not quite at home with a team of flies yet, but he felt sure that practice would take care of that. I wanted to fish with a single Peter Ross, but he would not hear of it.

The afternoon was pleasant, except that my bob fly seemed to have a life of its own, hooking everything but fish. James had fared rather better; he appeared with several good brown trout from the loch edge, but he was rather furtive with regard to what fly he had used, describing it as 'pinkish, a bit like a shrimp.' Most unfortunately he had mislaid the actual fly and was therefore not able to show it to Malcolm. However, having a suspicious mind, and remembering the picture in Peter Mackenzie-Philps' book under the heading 'The Pink Baby Doll Strikes Again' showing a wild brown trout from a Scottish loch with this florescent monstrosity firmly in the scissors, I demanded of my spouse "You didn't use a P.B.D. by any chance?" He had the grace to look guilty and made me promise not to tell Malcolm, who might consider it sacrilegious to use such a thing on his water. "But Peter was right, it worked, didn't it?"

On the second day I lost what felt like another good sea trout, together with my middle dropper - probably due to a wind-knot - which gave me the perfect excuse for leaving it off. The bob still regularly hooked everything with which it came into contact, including me. I took a brown trout on the point, and while I was playing it another came up and took the bob. After the initial surprise at finding myself playing two fish simultaneously I asked Malcolm what was the best thing to do, but the only reply I got was "Good question, Lassie." In netting the point fish the other kicked off, but there followed the usual tangle and unsnagging of hooks from the meshes of the net.

Malcolm had a nice basket of trout and James, having sneaked back to the junction of river and loch with his Willie Gunn, had taken another salmon and a brace of sea trout.

On our last day I was quite determined to master that bob fly and, helped by a much less boisterous wind, I managed reasonably well. Between us Malcolm and I had quite a respectable catch. We were about to reel in and make for the shore when I hooked a sea trout which, true to form, rushed about before coming towards the net. Here it gave one last desperate kick, and I felt the line go loose. I was sure that it had escaped, but suddenly all was tight again and the fish was still on, but behaving most oddly. When we got it into the net it was foul-hooked in the tail by the bob. It must have taken the Peter Ross on the point, rid itself of that hook and, in turning away, had encountered the Coch-y-bonddu.

James had also had quite a productive day and we all set off for home well pleased with ourselves. Malcolm did say that fishing with me seemed to be unusually eventful, there was never a dull moment. I'm not sure he meant it as a compliment.

Next morning James and I set off south after thanking our host for a wonderful three days. On the long drive home we agreed that it had been a most memorable visit to Scotland and that the fishing had been highly successful. But I have not fished with more than one fly on the cast since then, and the best I can conscientiously say of a bob fly is that you can have it.

Acknowledgments

Patricia Armstrong's short stories came to me via the golf course. She was contributing stories to 'Tales of Whortle Manor', a volume of golfing yarns built around an imaginary golf course. Her husband James had helped with the course design and during one of our conversations said, 'Of course, Pat's golf stories are not a patch on her fishing ones'.

My only experience with fishing had been on a lake in Canada's Nova Scotia in the early seventies. But I had several friends who were manic fishermen, I knew all fishermen love a good yarn, tall or otherwise, so I asked her to send the stories.

One of these friends, Graham 'Doc' Smith, recommended I send them to Bob Church, one of the sport's most respected names and himself an author of some note. He liked them, and offered some priceless advice. Then Charles Jardine, a household name in the world of fishing, offered to design the cover.

Pamela Joyce, meanwhile, had captured the mood of Patricia's stories with her sensitive black and white line drawings and Chris Poupard of the Salmon and Trout Association was full of enthusiasm for the book.

To all of the above, and to Paul Instrall's brilliant formatting, we are deeply grateful.

Ben Clingain
Editor
Northampton, May 1995